FLAT HOLM

FLAT HOLM
Bristol Channel
ISLAND

by Bob Jory and Friends

Featuring contributions from
John Barrett
David Benger
Lorna Gibson
Dr. John Guy
Rodney Legg
and **John Penny**

WINCANTON PRESS
NATIONAL SCHOOL, NORTH STREET
WINCANTON, SOMERSET BA9 9AT

Publishing details. First published in 1995, by the Wincanton Press, National School, North Street, Wincanton, Somerset BA9 9AT. Telephone: 01-963-32583.

Printing credits. Typeset and printed by F.W.B. Printing at Bennetts Mead, Southgate Road, Wincanton, Somerset BA9 9EB. Telephone: 01-963-33755.

Distribution. Nationally by Westcountry Books, Halsgrove House, Lower Moor Way, Tiverton Business Park, Tiverton, Devon EX16 6SS. Telephone: 01-884-243-242 Fax: 01-884-243-325 Locally, in South Wales, via Bob Jory, 19 Archer Terrace, Penarth, South Glamorgan CF64 3DU. Telephone: 01-222-709-400.

International standard book number [ISBN] 0 948699 50 7.

Contents

Break, break break,
On thy cold grey stones, O Sea!
And I would that my tongue could utter
The thoughts that arise in me.

Alfred, Lord Tennyson.

FOREWORD

by Alun Michael, Member of Parliament for
Cardiff South and Penarth.

Bob Jory's memoir of Flat Holm demonstrates once more the reasons why the island has such a powerful impact on the imagination of those who live on the South Wales Coast. There *is* a sense of magic — light and weather in the Seven Estuary play tricks so that one day the islands look gentle and distant while the next day they seem to have moved closer and loom larger. But the sense of history is explained by the tales in this book. The author's account takes us from the visitation of Breton pirates in 917 AD to the labours of feeding the first coal-fired lighthouse and the wartime role of the island between 1941 and 1944, when political in-fighting seems to have been a military priority! There is fascinating detail of the first radio transmissions across water between Flat Holm and Lavernock in 1897, but the people involved speak for themselves. The message from the first transmission on 3 May was passed to the Kaiser by his personal witness Professor Slaby — leaving us with a sense of curiosity: Why Wales? Why Lavernock? . . . Why not?

Emergencies such as the cholera epidemic, reflected in school records in Cardiff, show how much easier it is to plan for history than for the future, but throughout this memoir people are allowed to speak in their own voices. Arguments over whether air or sea targets are the priority during World War II, and the lifestyle of the time, could be used as the model for a new series which would combine the best of Dad's Army and The Good Life.

This is a memoir about *people* as well as an island.

PREFACE

I lived in Weston-super-Mare in the 1920s and often looked across to the islands of Steep Holm and Flat Holm, never thinking, but always hoping, that one day I would be able to visit them.

I can well remember the wonderful sunsets which were formed through the South Wales industrial haze. On still days steamships, and in those days they were numerous, left long trails of smoke which stayed until they were cleared by a favourable wind.

The history of Steep Holm has been covered in depth in several books, including *Allsop Island* (the island was purchased in memory of the naturalist and broadcaster Kenneth Allsop), *Steep Holm at War*, *Steep Holm Legends and History* and *Steep Holm Wild Life*, all by Rodney Legg, who has many books on Wessex to his credit.

I only hope that my collection of items about Flat Holm contained in this book will be of some interest.

Producing this book involved constant reference to various sources; in most instances these sources were my friends, and without their expert assistance it could not have been published. Therefore my grateful thanks go to the following:

John Barrett for information on the military occupation from 1869.

David Benger for his account of military life on the island during the Second World War.

Dr John Guy for his detailed history of the Cholera Hospital.

Quentin Clesham for his photographic reproductions.

Ingrid Emerson of the Flat Holm Project for access to Victorian photographs.

Lorna Gibson of Lundy for her chapter on the island flora and fauna.

Rodney Legg for his generous help and encouragement in the production and publishing of this book.

Alun Michael M.P., a busy man who kindly found time to prepare a foreword.

Trinity House Lighthouse Service for providing detailed information on the working of the island light.

G.E.C. Marconi Limited for allowing reproduction of George Kemp's diary of events at the time of the first transmission of wireless messages across water.

East Beach, with Wales in the background, drawn in 1988 by Lorna Gibson.

FLAT HOLM

The island of Flat Holm, composed of carboniferous limestone, lies in the Bristol Channel between Brean Down in the old county of Somerset, sometime known as Avon, and Lavernock in South Glamorgan. At one time the island, with Steep Holm, formed part of the Mendip Hills. It is shaped roughly like a plane leaf, in length from north to south approximately 550 metres, and in width from east to west approximately 475 metres. Until recently there was a considerable amount of ragwort covering the island and also a great number of elder bushes. Both to some extent have now been removed by the Flat Holm Project of South Glamorgan County Council,to whom the island is leased.

The earliest information regarding Flat Holm appears in the Parker manuscript of the Anglo-Saxon Chronicle under the year 917 AD, where we read:

"In this year a great pirate host came over hither from the south from Brittany under two jarls [noblemen next in dignity to a Scandinavian king, sometimes holding royal power but never assuming a kingly title], Ohtor and Hroald, and sailed west about until they reached the estuary of the Severn, and hamed at will everywhere along the Welsh coast. They seized Cyfeiliog, bishop of Archenfield [in Herefordshire — the name survives as that of a deanery] and took him with them to the ships, but King Edward ransomed him afterwards for forty pounds. Then after this the whole host went inland with the intention of renewing their raids in the direction of Archenfield: they were opposed by the men from Hereford and Gloucester and from the nearest fortresses who fought against them and put them to flight. They slew the jarl Hroald and the other jarl Ohtor's brother and a great part of the host, and drove them into an enclosure and besieged them there until they gave them hostages and promised to depart from King Edward's dominion.

"The king had arranged that the coast should be guarded along the southern shore of the Severn estuary, from Cornwall in the west eastwards as far as the mouth of the Avon, with the result that they durst not land anywhere in that region. However, they landed secretly by night on two separate occasions, once east of Watchet and again at Porlock, and on each occasion the English struck them so that only those few escaped who swam out to the ships. They encamped out on the island of Flatholm until the time came that they were very short of food, and many men perished of hunger, since they were unable to obtain provisions. They went thense to Dyfed [South Wales] and then out to Ireland, and this was in the autumn."

A further extract from the Anglo-Saxon Chronicle 1067 AD states: "In this year Gytha, mother of Harold, went out to the Isle of Flatholme and the wives of many good men accompanied her: she remained there for some time, and went thence oversea of St Omer." One wonders what shelter they had and how they were provisioned.

It is possible that the Scandinavian designation — Holm, for an estuarine island — dates from these earlier days, and it would have replaced the Saxon "Bradanreolice". There was probably an early monastic settlement, and a monastic site is shown on Ordnance Survey maps just to the north-east of what was the farmhouse, which is now somewhat altered and used as wardening accommodation.

On this site in 1942 extensive archaeological investigation was carried out by H.B.A. Ratcliffe-Densham, and the results were later published in Cardiff Naturalists' Society Transactions Vol. LXXX 1948-50.

Two graves were discovered on the monastic site, which were reputed to be those of the two murderers of Thomas à Becket, although there appeared to be no way of proving that this was so, and the culprits are credited with known graves elsewhere. Their legendary resting place on Flat Holm is situated some 25 yards to the east of the north-east corner of the old farmhouse. The north-western grave had plain head and foot stones of local limestone, and consisted of a low turf mound. A solid cube of rough limestone block was under the turf bound by old lime mortar, and was resting on a rubble of loam and broken stone roofing tiles, often perforated for plugs.

Removal of soil and rubble disclosed a grave with parallel head and foot, and sides that converged symmetrically towards the latter. The walls were built up of smooth, cut, tile-shaped limestone blocks, laid flat on one another and bound with soil. The floor was level and composed of large, flat, smooth limestone blocks. A circular hole, one foot in diameter, lay just to the west of the centre. The roof had been composed of similar blocks two inches thick, which rested on the flat tops of the side walls. The dimensions were: width at the head on the west end, 20 ins.; width on the east end, 11 ins.; length 6ft. 2ins.; depth covering slabs below ground surface, 2 ft. The wall had been damaged at the west end, and the roof had collapsed, filling the grave with rubble and earth.

The grave contained the greater part of a skeleton, but the skull, clavicles and some of the arm bones were missing. Above the level of the pelvis the bones were in extreme disorder, but those of the lower limbs were lying properly articulated. The feet were under the one covering slab which remained undisturbed; beside them was a small sherd of unglazed mediaeval pottery.

A second grave lay to the south-east of the one mentioned above, and had, lying beside it, a flat weathered covering slab of Purbeck stone. This was about four inches thick and five feet long, with parallel ends and chamfered converging sides, and was quite plain. This stone, unfortunately, is not in its original place. Over the last thirty years the writer has seen it in three different positions.

Excavation of the grave showed one and a half feet of loam and limestone rubble mixed with broken furniture, pantiles and modern china from the adjacent heap. Below was a coffin lid made of flat stone slabs perforated for bolts, of which serveral made of rusted iron were found. These stone fragments were in such disorder that it was impossible to determine whether the lid had originally consisted of one or more slabs.

Below these pieces were numerous human bones, mostly broken. They were lying in lime and appeared to represent the remains of two adult skeletons, one being a male. It was found impossible to build up one of the skulls, which was that a a well developed male of the modern type with good teeth.

As previously stated the information given above was taken from Volume 80 (1948-53) Transactions of the Cardiff Naturalists' Society, which gives further details of excavations carried out in 1942. A copy can be studied in the Cardiff Reference Library.

In 1542 the island was farmed by Edmond Turner, who had been granted a lease by the Crown. He was still holding it in 1551. In 1596 the Earl of Pembroke made an abortive claim to the rights, and sent one Thomas Wiseman to measure the farm. This we learn from a bailiff who wrote: "The flatt Holmes containeth lxj acre of errable and pasture lande and noe more, for I was p^{r}sent when Mr Mr Thomas Wiseman esquio^r measured the same by the commandem^t of my Lo: and Mr." Towards the end of the seventeenth century it was farmeed by Joseph Robins of Lavernock. His last will and testament reads as follows:

Joseph Robins of Lavernock, yeoman 1698 February 6.

To son Richard the messuage called Sutton's Farm, now in my possession, for the remainder of the term or lives.

To son Edward "all my right and title which I hold by vertue of one ch'ell Lease upon ye flatt holms with all priviledges and appurtenances thereof."
To daughter Jane Hawkins 2 heifers of 3 years old.
To son Richard "one young horse now grazeing upon ye flatt holms".

Further activities during the eighteenth century can be traced in Custom House letters and account books:

To Custom H^o Cardiff

Gentlemen,
Being inform'd that goods are run on a Sm^l Iseland called the fflat holmes within Bristol Channel And it Appearing that the King's Boat Station'd at Ely Ouze within your Port is near the said Holmes You are to order the officers belonging to the said Boat frequently to Visit this Iseland to prevent any frauds being committed there.

We are &c

John Hill
Robt Baylis
H. Hale

Custom h^o London
5° April 1735

To Custom H^o Cardiff

Gentlemen,
Having Rece'd Information that a Vessel is Dayly expected at the Flat Holmes who is to Come to an Anchor there at Night and send Her Goods Ashore by her Boat in order to be Concealed until opportunity offers to Carry them to other places We

Direct You to Communicate this Information to the Officers at y⁰ Port Barry and Sully and Direct them to use their utmost Endeavours to Prevent these frauds Reporting to us the Success

We are your Loving Friends

I Evelyn
I Stanley
C Piers
Robt Corbet

Custom h^o London
5 June 1735

1747

ffeb^{ry} To William Richards Surveyor going to Vissit the Iseland fflat Holms to see what Coals &c was landed there 5s

Dr. to Morgan Christopher for Assisting the Boatmen to bring up the K^s Boat from Pennarth (being so leaky) to be sent to Bristol 1s 6d

To John Jones Shipwright for Coming from Bonvilstone to View the said Boat and give his Judgm^t thereon 3s

To Wm Brewer for Carrying the s^d Boat Upon his Deck to Bristol — being to Leaky to be Towd 5s

Paid to Captn Priest for Bringing the New Kings Boat for Pennarth 5s.

1750

To Thomas Williams Extraman in Assisting the Boatmen at Pennarth in Rowing to the Holmes and Endeavouring to get there 13 6d

To said Thos Williams Attending the K^s Pennarth at sev^l times Rowland Vaughan having a Sore Leg 10s

1753

To Nich^s David Extraman to assist the Survey^r in Endeavouring to get to the fflat Holms but could not reach it, being 5 days at 1/6d per day 7s 6d.

Searchlight post and other war-works,
built in 1941–42, at Farmhouse Battery.
Drawn in 1988 by Lorna Gibson.

THE LIGHTHOUSE

The need for a lighthouse on the island had been discussed for many years by leading shipmasters and by members of the Society of Merchant Venturers of Bristol and in 1733 one John Elbridge, a senior member of the society, forwarded a petition to Trinity House, setting forth the dangers to navigation and the general desire for a light on the island.

In reply Elbridge was informed that no application had been made to the Crown for a light, that is, the signing of a petition by a substantial number of merchants of the post. At the same time the Corporation resolved to take measures to ensure that no light was erected other than in their name. All was quiet for the next two years, and in April 1735 William Crispe of Bristol informed Trinity House that he had leased Flat Holm Island for 99 years from John Stuart, Earl of Bute, and wished to build a lighthouse at his own expense, but in the name of the Corporation of Trinity House. Crispe may have demanded too high a toll, or possibly he was not prepared to lay out sufficient capital for the construction of a tower considered essential for an efficient light by the Society of Merchant Venturers. At their meeting on 9 May his scheme was rejected.

Towards the end of 1736 sixty soldiers were drowned when a vessel was wrecked near the Holms, and this gave added impetus for further negotiations to erect a light. On 17 March 1737 William Crispe attended at the Hall of Merchant Venturers with new proposals. The merchants then agreed to support a petition to Trinity House, and John Elbridge was asked to write to Admiral Sir Charles Wager [Master of Trinity House 1732-1737] stating that the merchants were prepared to subscribe to the light.

This new petition came before Trinity House on 2 April. In it Crispe stated that the Society of Merchant Venturers of Bristol would subscribe to pay for every vessel passing the light the following toll: "For all Bristol ships to or from foreign parts 1½d per ton both inward and outward, according to their reports of tonnage at the custom house, and double these dues on foreign ships. For all coasting vessels to or from Ireland 1d per ton: vessels from St David's Head or Lands End up the Bristol Channel (market boats and fishing boats excepted) one shilling for every voyage inward and one shilling outward."

The Merchant Venturers had insisted that Crispe should lay not less than £900 for the building of the tower. He agreed to this, and also that he would pay the expenses of Trinity House in obtaining the Crown patent for the light. In return he would expect to be granted a lease at a yearly rental of £5. The Corporation agreed at their next meeting on 9 April 1737 to apply for a patent and grant him a lease from the kindling of the light to Lady Day 1834, when the lease of the land expired, at a yearly rental of £5 for the first thirty years, and thereafter at £10 for the remainder of the term. The lease was finally signed on 3 September 1737. A light was first shown on 25 March 1738.

The light was coal fired, and as late as 1815 a Somerset surgeon, Dr Thomas Turner, spent a night at the island farmhouse, and later in his book *Memoir of Dr. Thomas Turner* gives us a good description of the light. The top was quite flat and about thirty feet in circumference, with cast iron railings around it. In the centre was a grate, six feet high and ten feet round with bars of a thickness of four inches. It seems that a half to three-quarters of a ton of coal was consumed by the light each night, all of which had to be carried up the steep winding staircase.

He states that the tower was surrounded by a high wall, forming a storage place for coal.

Owing to the increased cost of the structure William Crispe took into partnership one Benjamin Lund. However, their joint efforts were not sufficient, and a loan of £500 was secured from the previously mentioned John Elbridge. Again this was well below the necessary figure, and they were able to secure further loans of £700, £500 and £100 from Elbridge and one of £1,200 from Thomas Fane. In the same year of 1739 a further loan of £1,000 was obtained from a Mrs Susannah Heylyn.

John Elbridge died in 1739. He had not received payment of the loans, and the mortgage became part of his estate. The following year Crispe and Lund were bankrupt, and to clear their debts, passed their lease to Caleb Dickinson, in whose family it remained for three generations. Dickinson later accepted the post of collector of the dues of the Flat Holm light. He also had the management of the light, and kept the accounts. It seems that at this time thre were petty differences between Michael Richards, whose craft carried coal to the island, and a tenant-keeper of the light, Gilpin, who appeared to delight in creating difficulties wherever possible.

In October 1744 Richards wrote to the ship owners that after a most difficult trip to the island, Gilpin refused to accept the coal, complaining that the landing stage was already full of coal, and therefore requested from them a further fifteen shillings for his "extraordinary expenses". On another occasion he managed to be away from the island when Richards arrived, and so the craft had to return to the mainland fully laden.

Some two years later Gilpin was drowned leaving Barry harbour on his return to the island. After this his widow continued to farm the island and tended the light but acted in the same unpleasant manner towards Michael Richards, in the first instance complaining about the quality of the coal. Richards also complained that she had offered his brother half a guinea to swear that Bristol coal was better than that obtained from Cardiff. Unfortunately the boat became so unseaworthy that the crew refused to take her to sea, and supplies were obtained from Bristol, Richards's final comment about his men being: "it is too troublesome to have to deal with a Sett of Animals who are as difficult to keep in order as the waves they go upon".

Thomas Biss who was then an assistant keeper stated that Mrs Gilpin "drank so much liquor that she did not know what she did". She was later removed from the island, and her place taken by Biss.

On the night of 22 December 1790 during a fierce gale the Lighthouse was struck by lightning, and to quote the keeper's report: "We expected every moment to be our last. At three o'clock in the morning of the 23rd the tower was struck by lightning. The man attending the fire was knocked down and narrowly escaped falling through the stairway. The iron fire grate was smashed to pieces and the top of the tower considerably damaged."

While repairs took place a fire was maintained on the headland near the lighthouse. An existing lime kiln was brought into use for the making of the mortar, and was fired from existing fuel stocks. This kiln may still be seen near the shore to the west of the farmhouse.

In 1819 the height of the lighthouse was increased by twenty feet to ninety feet. On this a ten foot lantern was constructed. This housed a new type of oil burner, designed by the French inventor Argand in 1784. This fixed white light was first shown on 7 September 1820. By an Act of Parliament passed in 1821 Trinity House became empowered to purchase outright the leases on any coastal lights, and in 1836 were able to purchase any lights remaining in private ownership. In the case of Flat Holm light, this was carried out on 21 March 1823. In 1867 new lenses were installed which are still in existence.

In 1881 the fixed light was removed and replaced by an occulting light, timed as follows: eclipse three seconds; light three seconds; eclipse three seconds; light twenty-one seconds. In 1969 the 100mm petroleum vapour burner was removed, and an electric light installed. Since then the characteristics have flashed three times every ten seconds.

Until 12 May 1988 three keepers were in attendance, but on this date the light became fully automatic and sadly they left.

The Trinity House lighthouse service have kindly supplied comprehensive information on the present system and this is included in full.

1739   1820   1866

FLATHOLM LIGHTHOUSE Glamorgan

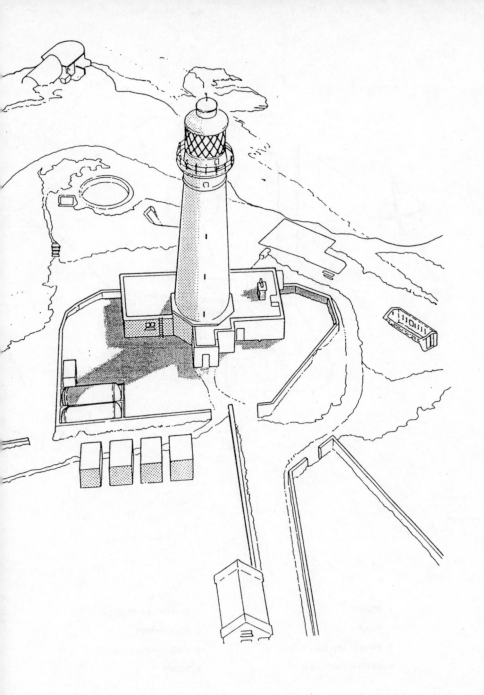

Flatholm Lighthouse

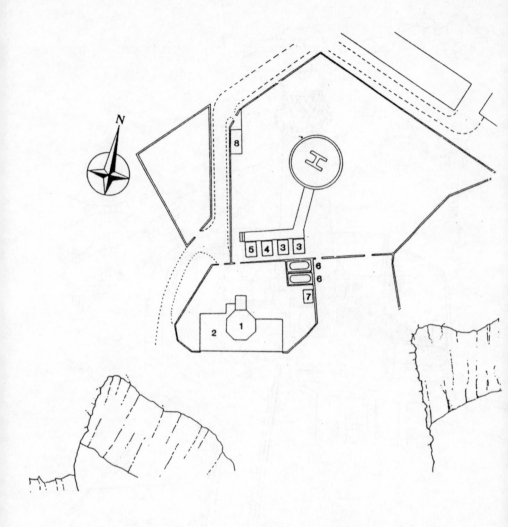

1. TOWER

2. TOWER BASE

3. ENGINE MODULES

4. BATTERY MODULE

5. EQUIPMENT MODULE

6. FUEL TANKS

7. FUEL CUBICLE

8. STORE

Fig 1   Site Plan, Flatholm Lighthouse

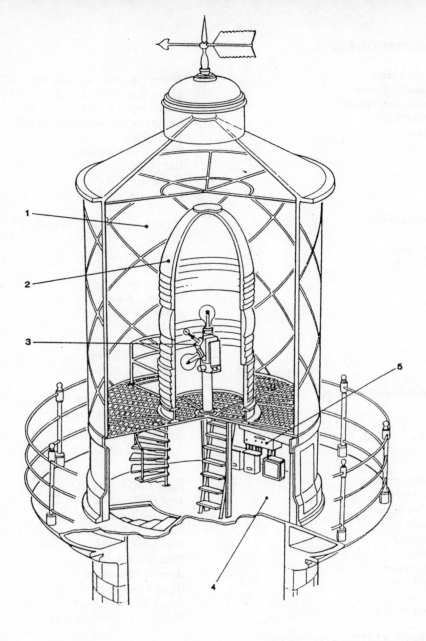

1. Lantern Room
2. Optic Lens
3. Navigation Light 3-position Changer
4. Service Room
5. Navigation Light Control Cubicle

Service Room

NAVIGATION LIGHT

Main Lamp	Thorn type EC111A, 240 V ac 3 kW
Standby Lamp	Thorn type EC111A, 240 V ac 3 kW
Emergency Lamp	Thorn type L3, 50 V dc 250 W
Lampchanger	Stone Chance 3-position, Mk II
Optic	1st Order
	920 mm focal length
	Catadioptric
	Fixed lens 360 deg
	Horizontal aperture
Character	Flash 3 white/red 10 seconds
Analysis	Flash 1 sec
	Eclipse 1.5 sec
	Flash 1 sec
	Eclipse 1.5 sec
	Flash 1 sec
	Eclipse 4 sec
Intensity	White 30 500 candelas
	Red 25 000 candelas
IALA Nominal Range	White 17 Nautical miles
	Red 16 Nautical miles

FOG SIGNAL

Manufacturer	Automatic Power Ltd.
Emitters	4 off ELG 500
Drive units	2 CG 1000 inverters
Coder unit	Dual CG 1000 timer
Detector	AGA type FD300
Signal	Twin 5 in sirens
Character	Horn of 30 seconds
Analysis	Blast 3 sec
	Silent 27 sec
Range	Better than 4 Nautical miles

DIESEL ALTERNATOR SETS

Manufacturer	Hawker Siddeley Marine
Engine	Lister TS3 18 BHP
Alternator	Mawdsley type 2D A4KB + 7B16N
Output	10 kW at 0.8 PF
	240 volts single phase
	50 Hz.

BATTERY CHARGERS

Manufacturer	Harmer & Simmons Ltd.
Tower base	Type TC 1A 50/30 (1)
	Output: float 50 V nominal
	Boost: 54.48 V
Battery module	Type TC 1A 24/30 (3)
	Output: float 24 V nominal
	Boost: 33 V
Engine modules	Type ER 24/12 (2)
	Output: 24 V, 12 A rating

BATTERIES

Manufacturer	Tungstone Batteries Ltd.
Emergency light	24 cells type HBP 33
Engine	12 cells type HBP 7
Radio	12 cells type HBP 25
Fog control	12 cells type HBP 25
Equipment control	12 x 2 type HAP 5
Emergency domestic light	12 cells type HBP 25

RADIO/TELEMETRY

VHF radios	
Shore to shore/ship	Sailor VHF R/T
	Type RT 144/C
Helicopter link	Park Air
Telemetry	Trend/system Racal Vodaphone
	radio/telephone link

FAN UNITS

Towerbase battery room	
Manufacturer	Vent-Axia
	Type S9RF SAR
Equipment module	
Manufacturer	Zeihl - EBM (UK) Ltd.
	Type G2E 108 AA01 - 50
Battery module	
Manufacturer	Zeihl - EBM (UK) Ltd.
	Type G2E 108 AAO1 - 50
	A K Fans Ltd.
Manufacturer	Type LF X4562
Engine module	
Manufacturer	Air Filter Services Ltd.
	Type SD6-770-E650-4

EQUIPMENT

Services

1.   The principal services and power supplies for Flatholm Lighthouse are separately housed in four steel modules situated close to the tower base entrance. These are designated Equipment Module, Battery Module, Engine A and Engine B Modules.

2.   Fuel for the diesel/alternator sets is contained in two tanks adjacent to the engine modules.

Navigation Light

3.   The main and standby navigation lights are identical 240 V - 3000 W lamps carried on a three-position lamp changer which is mounted on a pedestal in the lantern room. Normally the main lamp is in the focussed position, but in the event of main lamp failure, the lamp changer arm pivots through 135 degrees to bring the standby lamp into the focussed position. The character of the light is governed by coders and the exhibiting period is 24 hours continuous.

4.   In addition to automatic operation, remote control is available from the Base Control Station at Nash Point, and local control from the navigation lights control cubicle and station supervisor unit.

Emergency Light

5.   The emergency light is a 50 V - 250 W lamp located equidistant between the main and standby lamps on the lamp changer arm. The emergency lamp is rotated into the focussed position by automatic operation of the lamp changer motor.

Fog Signal

6.   Four electric fog signal emitters are located on the exterior wall of the tower. The fog signal control system is situated in the Equipment Module and power is supplied from the main diesel/alternator set. In the automatic mode the sounding of the fog signal is determined by a fog detector positioned in the lantern room of the tower. The character of the signal is governed by the fog signal coder.

7.   Remote control is available from the base control station at Nash Point, and local control from the station supervisor unit.

AUTOMATIC MODE OPERATION

Navigation Light

19.   Current mode of operation is that the main navigation light is exhibiting 24 hours a day. Two time switches are available to vary the exhibiting period but they are permanently switched to the 'off' position.

20.   If the main lamp should fail for any reason, the standby lamp is automatically rotated into the focussed position and switched on.

Fog Signal

21.   When the fog detector senses fog conditions, it will activate the fog signal equipment. The signal emitters will continue sounding until the detector senses clear conditions. If any of the 4 emitters fail, the other three continue to sound the signal. If all four emitters fail or if the ac supply fails, there is no standby power supply and the signal is not sounded. The fog detector is 'fail safe' and if it is damaged or faulty the fog signal will sound automatically, even in clear conditions.

22.   The fog signal control system contains a heating system control cubicle. The control unit is an integral part of the heating system circuit and, to avoid an overload situation developing when the fog signal is sounding, it disconnects the heaters when the emitters are activated. The heaters are reconnected when the emitters stop sounding, this sequence of events proceeds until the fog detector senses clear conditions and de-activates the fog signal.

Power Supplies

23.   In the automatic mode the main diesel/alternator set (Module A) runs on line. If the diesel stops for any reason or a fault develops in the alternator power output, the standby set (Module B) automatically starts up to maintain continuity of the electrical supply, and simultaneously an 'alarm' signal is transmitted to base control at Nash Point. The standby diesel/alternator set will continue to run until the fault is corrected in the main set.

24.   If both diesel/alternator sets fail, the emergency lamp and supply system automatically comes into operation.

Remote Control

25.   The control equipment at Nash Point monitors the signals transmitted by the telemetry control equipment of Flatholm continuously. If a fault is detected, it is signalled to the Supervisor Unit at Nash Point (which controls both Flatholm and Mumbles telemetry links) and the appropriate action can then be taken. Full details of this equipment and the control procedure is contained in a separate handbook for the Nash Point Control Room.

Main and Standby Electrical Generation

8.   The ac supply for all the station services is provided by two diesel/alternator sets operating as main and standby units. The diesel/alternator sets are housed in Modules A and B, set A usually being designated as the main unit. Each set is fully independent of the other, with its own fuel system and starter supply.

9.   If required, the standby (Module B) diesel/alternator set can be started-up and brought on-line manually under local control, or via the command link from base control.

10.   An independent small diesel/generator set located in the tower base generator room can be started locally to provide a domestic supply if required.

Emergency Electrical Supplies

11.   A 24 V dc supply to maintain emergency operation of the Equipment Module is available from the Battery Module, and a 50 V dc supply for the emergency navigation light is available from the Battery Room in the tower base.

12.   All batteries are continuously float-charged by the operating diesel/alternator set.

Fuel Oil System

13.   Fuel oil for the diesel engines is stored in two 6820 litre GRP storage tanks adjacent to the diesel/alternator modules. The diesel engines are gravity fed from the storage tanks, each engine taking its supply from one associated tank making in effect two independent fuel supply systems.

Radio Communications

14.   A Sailor VHF transmitter/receiver for Station-to-Ship/Shore radio communications, and a Park Air VHF for Station-to-Helicopter contact are provided. Both are situated in the lobby of the tower base. A vodaphone radio handset is provided in the Equipment Module for communication and telemetry supervision with Base Control at Nash Point.

Remote Control and Monitoring

15.   The Trend control units at Flatholm monitor the station functions; all alarms are reported to Nash Point Control via Vodaphone link.

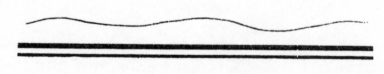

THE ISLAND AT WAR

At the outbreak of the Franco-Prussian War there were rumours that war between France and Britain was imminent, and Viscount Palmerston, the Prime Minister, appointed Sidney Herbert as his Secretary of War.

As early as 1856 the island was considered for use as part of the coast artillery defences of the Bristol Channel and Severn Estuary. During 1865, nine acres of land was purchased from the Marquis of Bute for £550. In 1869 one additional acre was leased from Trinity House at a rent of one shilling per annum. Construction of the gun batteries began about 1866. Due to the relatively low and exposed terrain Moncrieff disappearing batteries were installed; none of the special carriages remain.

The barracks, dated "VR 1869" over the main entrance, provided accommodation for about fifty men, but only a master gunner and five gunners were stationed there. Once a year the vicar and curate of St Mary's, Cardiff, visited the island and held a service in the barracks. A commercial photographer visited the island about 1875 to photograph the lighthouse. He selected a view which included a gun pit and the barracks. Seeing that the gun was in the down position and wishing to add interest in the foreground, he asked a gunner to raise it, which he did. When the photograph later came to the notice of the military authorities it was immediately suppressed and the unfortunate gunner reprimanded.

Armament consisted of nine RML (Rifled Muzzle Loading) guns made at the Royal Gun Foundry, Woolwich Arsenal, mounted in four separate batteries all in Montcrieff pits. These are constructed of limestone blocks and bricks; they are 18 feet in diameter and ten feet deep; some are linked by underground passages and magazines. During World War II many were used, but some were covered over and generator beds mounted.

31

Castle Rock Battery was armed with three RML guns, two in circular pits and one in an open back pit. One gun has been removed and the other two have been cut up, leaving just the breach which is marked with the number RM10 - HS.

Lighthouse Battery was the most important position; it is surrounded by a steep cliff and a 20 feet wide dry defensive moat which protected the battery, barracks and supporting buildings. Three guns were mounted; one of the pits has an open back. All the guns are complete but with some surface corrosion, one is dated 1869. Under a grassy mound near the Lighthouse is a large underground magazine or store. If the island had been overwhelmed by an attacking force, gun detachments could have fallen back to the Lighthouse Battery.

Farmhouse Battery is on the western coast overlooking the sea. This site was equipped with two RML guns in separate pits. All that remains of the guns are two sections of breech, one of which shows a Victorian crest. The fabric of both pits is intact.

Well Battery was installed on the coast between the Lighthouse and the farmhouse. The open back pit remains and its single gun is the subject of an interesting story. The gun remained on Flat Holm until 1963 when the Army Apprentices College at Chepstow decided to remove it and place it on a mock wooden carriage outside their college guardroom. During September 1963 stage one of the recovery from the battery began. Staff Sergeant T. Crane, R.E. and apprentices 61A and 62C, 'A' Company transported the gun to the landing beach. As it was being rolled down the path it toppled over, injuring the hand of an apprentice, and it fell on to the beach, where it remained until stage two of the recovery. Final recovery and transportation by boat was carried out by the apprentices to intake 62B 'A' company during the late summer of 1964. Well Battery has the highest known recorded serial number, "RGF No 100 III 1869".

The author is indebted to Mr J.H. Barrett for permitting the inclusion of the detailed information on the old island gun batteries, taken from his *A History of Maritime Forts in the Bristol Channel 1866-1900.*

WARTIME LIFE ON THE ISLAND

The island played no part in the First World War but was the scene of considerable activity during the Second World War. A survey was made in September 1940 when it was decided to mount two batteries of two 4.5 inch dual purpose anti-aircraft and anti-ship guns and two searchlights. It was considered inadvisable to mount the guns in the old gun pits. These were very deep, and were utilised as watch shelters. By 23 September 1941 two guns were mounted on the south site and became operational soon afterwards. The emplacements for these guns were not begun, however, until a year later. The north site became operational in December 1942. The guns were sited to defend the north and middle channels of the Bristol Channel and to prevent enemy E-boats passing the line Steep Holm — Flat Holm — Lavernock. The Fort had primarily a "Close Defence" role, but could be used for long ranges up to 20,000 yards. The secondary role was anti-aircraft, two 40mm Bofors, one twin Lewis and four Lewis guns being mounted. The batteries were from the 570 Coast Regiment Royal Artillery, 205 Coast Battery Royal Artillery on the north site, and 146 Coast Battery Royal Artillery on the south. The island became non-operational on 18 December 1944.

Some years ago the writer was fortunate enough to meet Major David Benger, an island Battery Commander during the Second World War, who after a nostalgic visit wrote two interesting accounts of wartime life on the island. These are now reproduced in full.

MONCRIEFF CARRIAGE

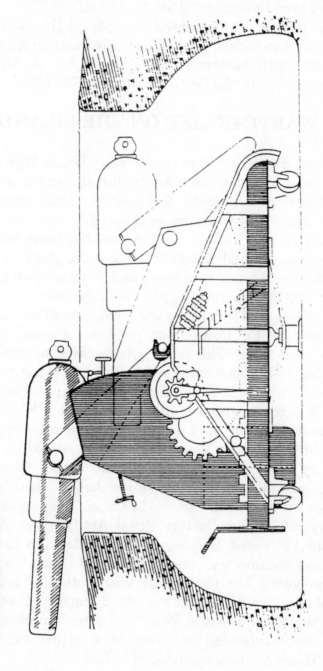

WITH 7 INCH R.M.L. GUN

The drawing shows both the raised firing position, and the recoiled position down in the gun-pit where the cannon was loaded in relative safety.

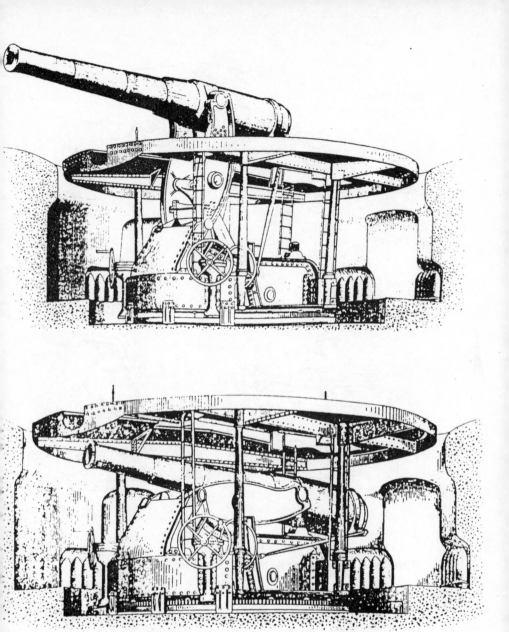

Hydropneumatic mounting for a disappearing gun, as issued to Flat Holm in 1871.

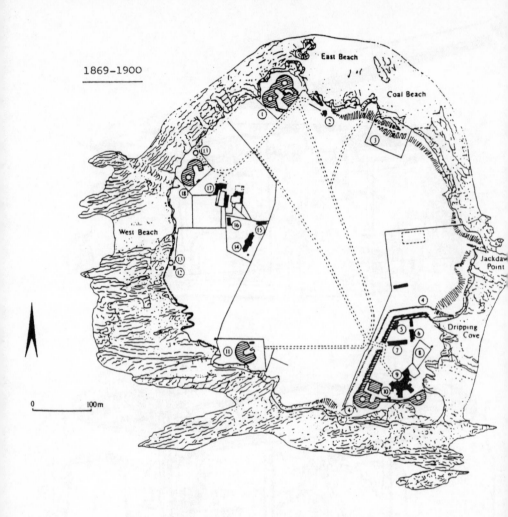

A plan of the island during the first military occupation.

1. Castle Rock Battery.
2. Store house.
3. Site of fifth battery not constructed.
4. Defensive ditch.
5. Secure building.
6. Administrative building.
7. Barracks.
8. Water catchment area.
9. Lighthouse and surrounding buildings.
10. Lighthouse Battery.
11. Well Battery.
12. Crematorium.
13. Lime kiln.
14. Cholera Hospital.
15. Second ward and doctor's accommodation.
16. Laundry.
17. Farmhouse.
18. Farmhouse Battery.

GERMAN FIELD RAILWAY

by Rodney Legg

As a member of the United Kingdom Fortifications Club told military historian Peter D. Cobb, on Steep Holm in 1983: "If word got around, this would soon become a Mecca for light railway buffs."

Cobb and the others understood why. For both Steep Holm and Flat Holm have surviving lengths of German Wehrmacht 60 centimetre gauge Feld Bahn railway with British modifications, which on Steep Holm were to turn it from its previous horizontal use into a cliffside incline railway. That on Flat Holm was used conventionally. Together the two islands show just about the full gambit of usage possibilities.

"The very gauge itself is historically interesting," Cobb told me — as he pointed out that the un-English 1 foot 11½ inches was explained by the fact that it was continental 60 centimetres. "The total length of extant sections, including the amount on Flat Holm, is a significant portion of the 70 kilometres captured from the Germans on the Western Front between 1916 and 1918, and added to in the 1919 reparations."

This was the standard German Field Railway and was used extensively between and behind their lines to bring up guns, ammunition, stores, personnel and just about all the materiel from the main rail-head depots to the front-line trenches.

The total of 70 kilometres that was acquired and shipped to England by the British Army was divided into two lengths of 35 kilometres. These were then stacked in stores at Chattenden near Rochester, Kent, and at the Longmoor Railway Depot, between Liphook and Liss, near Petersfield, in Hampshire.

Amateur historians have been deceived as to its Wehrmacht origins by the subsequent ingenious grafting, to the German base-stock, of various British-made fittings. These were ordered from the sewerage and mineworking industries and include cable wheels and rail-switching levers. Cable traction on Steep Holm was by both electrical power and hand winching.

Guns, including both anti-aircraft and the bigger 6-inch anti-ship weapons, were moved and emplaced on both islands by use of the railway, as Cyril Stickland recalled for me. The islands were fortified in 1941 for the Fixed Defences Severn, specifically to defend the Atlantic convoy de-grouping zone off Cardiff, and the South Wales ports.

On Steep Holm one of the former naval guns, now in the hands of the Royal Artillery, slipped off the rails and had to be recovered from its landing place on the almost precipitous eastern cliffs. It has left gouges in the rail near the top of that island's second incline.

"Most of the work had to be done at night," Stickland told me in 1991. That was to avoid presenting the Luftwaffe with an irresistible target. "Then we couldn't have any light to work by, we daren't."

Members of the 930 Port Construction Company of the Royal Engineers, who fortified Flat Holm and Steep Holm in the late summer of 1941, told me that the laying of the railways was the first work to be done. On Steep Holm they had to blast out the necessary inclines from the cliffs. Flat Holm came easier, though in both cases oxyacetyline torches and a mandrill were used to make a few modifications to match the gradient profile.

It is ironical that a creation of German industry for their forces in one war would be brought out and used against them by our side in the next.

Numerous railway wheels and rusting sections of their trucks survive on the two islands. Those little wagons, arguably, were also German. "Ours were always wooden around the sides," a Purbeck clay-mine foreman told me. "For yours to be all-metal they have to be continental; we never saw anything this modern in the West Country until the 1970s."

Some of the Steep Holm relics survive and have been smartened, courtesy military writer John Barrett and Hammerite paints, with Bristol scouts taking on some equipment in situ. That said, their longer term preservation verges on the impossible. All wartime metalwork, on both islands, is rusting into history and oblivion.

What can be done should be done, Peter Cobb emphasised. "Please tell your trustees and the councillors who run Flat Holm that very few examples of this ex-German Field Railway now exist in the United Kingdom. It is to be hoped that the trustees of both islands will try and preserve as much of their unique systems as possible."

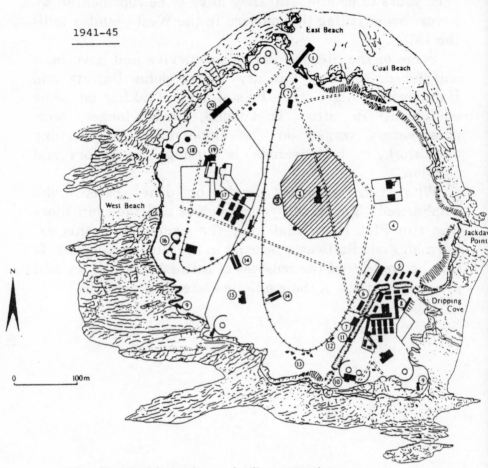

A plan of the island during the second military occupation.

1. Pier.
2. Railway terminus.
3. Gun Laying mark 2 radar platform and false horizon.
4. Water tower.
5. Sergeants' mess and lines.
6. Guard house.
7. Gas attack store.
8. Other ranks' lines.
9. Searchlight housing.
10. Command post: South Battery.
11. Royal Electrical and Mechanical Engineers workshops.
12. Battery charging unit.
13. South Battery.
14. Magazine.
15. Command Post: North Battery.
16. North Battery.
17. N.A.A.F.I., kitchens, dining halls, library and post office.
18. Generator, and air raid siren.
19. Officers' mess.
20. Hospital.

WAR DIARY
OF THE ISLANDS

Research by John Penny
Words by Rodney Legg

September 1940: Reconnaissance of Flat Holm.

7 October 1940: Report recommends inclusion of Flat Holm in a "Severn North Fire Command" with two 4-inch guns to be installed at Farmhouse Battery and another pair at Lighthouse Battery.

March 1941: Bristol Channel Coastal Defence Artillery established by Southern Command, with a plan for twelve 6-inch guns to be emplaced in the Bristol Channel Scheme. The recommendation is for immediate priority to be given to preparing sites at once for two 6-inch batteries (each with two guns) on Flat Holm. The strategic purpose is to provide and protect a de-grouping zone for Atlantic convoys awaiting dock space and suitable tides for entering the South Wales ports.

30 May 1941: 2nd Lieutenant I.T. Goodchild and five other ranks of 29 (Railway Survey) Company of the Royal Engineers, sent on detachment from Leeds to Barry Island to survey work proposed for Flat Holm and Steep Holm, on behalf of the War Office.

13 June 1941: Bristol Channel Defence Artillery fire their first shot in semi-anger, at 07.00 hours from Nell's Point, Barry. A small tanker, seen at 195 degrees and about 1,700 yards by 130 Coast Battery, fails to hoist signals. One "bring to" round is fired but the vessel fails to stop and disappears into the mist. Later identified as steamship *Overton*, heading for Burnham-on-Sea.

30 June 1941: 166 Pioneer Company moved from Hayes Lane Camp, Barry Docks, to Wenvoe Camp, to prepare for deployment on Flat Holm and Steep Holm.

4 July 1941: 930 Port Construction and Repair Company of the Royal Engineers begin the fortification of Flat Holm, under the command of Major D.P. Bertlin. The 300-ton coastal steamer *Assurity*, owned by Everards of Greenhithe, arrives with an advance party. Their company headquarters has been established at 42 Redbrink Crescent, Barry Island. *Assurity* sailed from Barry Docks at 10.00 hours.

5 July 1941: *Assurity* returns to Flat Holm with stores. A camp has been set up and the old Cholera Hospital is being turned into a messing room, kitchen, and recreation room. The old Laundry will be a detachment office and the lower section of the Lighthouse is to be converted into an officers' mess.

6 July 1941: *Assurity* brings more stores to Flat Holm and Major Bertlin on a visit there and to Steep Holm. Base stores for both units are being gathered in a Stores Dump at Ping Pong Sidings, Barry Dock.

7 July 1941: *Assurity* again arrives with stores and takes an advance party of one N.C.O. and twelve men, from Flat Holm, to establish a camp on Steep Holm. Work has commenced on a "T-head" pier at Flat Holm.

8 July 1941: Sand, steelwork, and cement delivered to Flat Holm. *Assurity* brought steel girders for jetty-building. She was driven as far up the beach as possible and her load removed as the tide ebbed. Emergency rations for seven days are landed on Steep Holm.

9 July 1941: Government motor launch brings Major Bertlin to visit his detachments at Flat Holm, Steep Holm, and the Somerset mainland fortifications on Brean Down.

12 July 1941: Thirty men from 116 Company of the Pioneer Corps, attached to 930 Port Construction and Repair Company, are brought to Flat Holm by *Assurity*.

13 July 1941: Despite heavy storms, motor launch *Wanderer* brings Major Bertlin and Captain McLeod from Barry, on a tour of duty to Flat Holm and Steep Holm.

15 July 1941: Stormy again, with a rough sea. Sergeant Rock of 930 Port Construction and Repair Company left Barry at 17.00 hours on Royal Navy Paddle Steamer *New Roseland* to deliver stores at Steep Holm and Flat Holm. From Steep Holm they embarked three men who were to be conveyed to Flat Holm. They were.3379057 Sergeant John Harwood; 1057223 Corporal Goffton Cyril Bull; and 101668 Sapper W.B. Moyse. Whilst disembarking off Flat Holm, in a choppy sea, the dinghy capsized and the three were drowned. Major Bertlin recalled this incident for Rodney Legg in 1977: "We very tragically lost three men whom the Navy, at my request, attempted to land on Flat Holm. They were put into a dinghy with the idea that they should be towed ashore. The dinghy collapsed and all three men were immediately drowned as they were encumbered by military equipment. The seaman rowing them, being without equipment, was saved. My officer, Hopper, awaiting them on shore, was powerless to do anything to help."

19 July 1941: Sergeant and 32 other ranks of 116 Pioneer Company arrive on Steep Holm to navvy for 930 Port Construction and Repair Company.

21 July 1941: The body of Sapper Moyse, who was drowned off Flat Holm, has been recovered near Sully Island. [He is buried in Sunderland.]

22 July 1941: Corporal Bull's body has been washed up at Portishead. [He is buried in the town.]

25 July 1941: Visits to Flat Holm and Steep Holm by men of the Royal Corps of Signals, to establish radio stations to work with the shore station at Barry Island.

26 July 1941: The body of Sergeant Harwood, the third victim of the Flat Holm drownings, has been recovered from the sea at Weston-super-Mare. [He is buried there.]

29 July 1941: Radio communications now operational between Nell's Point, Barry Island, and the Royal Engineers on Flat Holm and Brean Down.

31 July 1941: Radio communication to Steep Holm also established from Nell's Point.

1 August 1941: Excavation work for a "T-head" quay on the beach at Steep Holm completed. Erection of superstructure commenced.

3 August 1941: Instructions received from the War Office to construct a tramway up the eastern side of Steep Holm.

5 August 1941: Orders received to cease work on pier construction at Brean Down and transfer No.3 Section of

930 Port Construction and Repair Company from there to Steep Holm.

6 August 1941: First civilian contractors arrive on Flat Holm and are to be accommodated separately from the military camp.

14 August 1941: "T-head" quay construction complete on Flat Holm, with the exception of the "L4" trestles on top. Lieutenant R.F. Spoule replaces Lieutenant Forbes, in command of the contingent from 116 Pioneer Company.

17 August 1941: All available labour has now been concentrated on the blasting and making of an incline tramway up the hillside on Steep Holm.

25 August 1941: Supply hitch in the transport of materials to Steep Holm and Flat Holm due to the barge *Yumbi* sustaining damage.

30 August 1941: All materials required to complete the work of 930 Port Construction and Repair Company, on both Flat Holm and Steep Holm, have now been delivered to the respective islands.

6 September 1941: Advance party from No.4 Section, 690 General Construction Company of the Royal Engineers, embark from Barry Dock for Steep Holm. Commanded by Leading-Sergeant Rogers.

7 September 1941: The jetty at Flat Holm has been completed and only twenty men of 930 Port Construction and Repair Company now remain on the island.

8 September 1941: Remainder of No.4 Section, 690 General Construction Company, embark from Barry Dock for Steep Holm at 05.30 hours.

9 September 1941: No.1 Section, 690 General Construction Company sail from Barry Dock to Flat Holm, at 06.30 hours, under Second-Lieutenant Fitzgerald.

10 September 1941: No.3 Section 690 General Construction Company leave Barry Dock for Steep Holm, at 07.00 hours, under Captain Smith. No.2 Section then left for Flat Holm at 07.30 hours. They have come from Wenvoe Camp, near Cardiff. Reinforcements of 100 other ranks from 116 Pioneer Company sent with them, mainly to work on the rail-road up the cliff-face.

17 September 1941: First two 4.5 inch dual purpose guns and predictors landed at West Beach, Flat Holm. Plans for Flat Holm were modified, at the request of Anti-Aircraft Command, to provide an offshore contribution to the air defence of Cardiff, as well as the anti-E-boat capacity originally intended. The 6-inch anti-ship guns were to go to Steep Holm instead. Flat Holm North (military map reference 110/660863) was emplaced with two 4.5-inch dual role anti-aircraft/anti-ship guns to an arc of fire 360 degrees, west, to 160 degrees. Approximate range 6,000 yards. Flat Holm South (military map reference 110/662860) was similarly provided with two 4.5-inch dual role guns of similar range, with an arc of fire from 320 degrees, west to 115 degrees.

18 September 1941: The two upper legs of the incline tramway up to the top of the cliff on Steep Holm have been completed. Work has now been resumed on the pier. Only six men of 930 Port Construction and Repair Company remain on Flat Holm. Generators and projectors have been landed there.

19 September 1941: The remaining two 4.5-inch dual purpose guns and predictors are landed on Flat Holm.

20 September 1941: A Tank Landing Craft has arrived at Barry Docks to convey the four 6-inch guns to Steep Holm.

21 September 1941: Unsuccessful attempt at landing 6-inch guns, equipment, and mules on Steep Holm.

24 September 1941: Mules landed on Steep Holm.

25 September 1941: Winches now installed on Flat Holm and two 4.5-inch guns have been mounted at the South Site. They will soon be operational but are not yet protected by emplacements.

26 September 1941: Jetty foundations completed at Flat Holm and Steep Holm.

28 September 1941: 930 Port Construction and Repair Company begins to withdraw machinery and tools from Flat Holm. Second-Lieutenant Moffat and Sapper Browne of 690 General Construction Company arrive on Steep Holm to set out Nissen huts. Three sections of 116 Pioneer Company now on Steep Holm and two sections on Flat Holm.

30 September 1941: After much delay and difficulty two 6-inch naval guns, plus a generator and equipment, have now been landed at Steep Holm. 930 Port Construction and Repair Company strength is now as follows. Barry — two officers and 69 other ranks. Plus twelve other ranks in a working party from the Royal Artillery. Steep Holm — two officers and 68 other ranks. Plus 48, average, other ranks from the Pioneer Corps, together with two from the Royal Artillery and one man from the Royal Army Medical Corps. Flat Holm — one officer and seven other ranks.

1 October 1941: The remaining two 6-inch naval guns have been landed on Steep Holm.

2 October 1941: The lighter *Yumbi* was inundated and has sunk, whilst en route to Steep Holm, with all cement being lost.

6 October 1941: 20.50 hours. A Junkers Ju.88 bomber has dropped a mine in the sea between Steep Holm and Brean Down.

7 October 1941: Trestling completed for the jetty at Steep Holm. At 20.45 hours a Junkers Ju.88 bomber of III Gruppe, Kampfgeschwader 30, flying from Melun in France, dropped a mine on Flat Holm. Equipment and buildings were damaged and a total of 29 men injured by flying glass. Barry Docks has been closed to shipping.

8 October 1941: Rail winches installed in tramway "laybys" on Steep Holm. Medical stores dropped on Flat Holm, by an aircraft, at 18.00 hours.

9 October 1941: Barry Docks still closed to outgoing vessels. Admiralty orders require the launch *Corrigoyle* to be armed to go to Flat Holm to fetch the casualties. 10.00 hours — more medical stores dropped on Flat Holm from the air.

10 October 1941: Ports re-opened at 12.30 hours. *Corrigoyle* attempts to reach Flat Holm and Steep Holm but adverse tides and rough sea prevented landing on the latter. Five serious casualties have been evacuated from Flat Holm. The motor launch *Peter Piper* also reached Flat Holm with rations but *Assurity*, detailed for Steep Holm, did not sail from Barry as the skipper could not be found. Situation on Steep Holm, with regard to rations, now regarded as serious. There are only four days' reserve rations and little water.

11 October 1941: Further rations delivered to Flat Holm.

12 October 1941: No.2 Section of 930 Port Construction and Repair Company withdrawn from both Steep Holm and Flat Holm.

13 October 1941: Winter clothing and mail reach Flat Holm.

16 October 1941: Timber jetty completed at Flat Holm. Rations are at last delivered to Steep Holm.

17 October 1941: Ladders fixed to jetty on Flat Holm.

19 October 1941: Launch landed at Flat Holm but it proved impossible to take Captain Smith of 690 General Construction Company off the island. His dinghy was swamped and the oars lost.

20 October 1941: 11.00 hours. Launch fetches Captain Smith from Flat Holm. 189 Coastal Battery has been incorporated in 531 Regiment of the Royal Artillery, formerly part of 524 Coast Regiment, for deployment at the North Site on Steep Holm (Summit Battery).

21 October 1941: Mooring rings fixed into the rocks around the jetty on Flat Holm.

29 October 1941: Laying of timber decking on Steep Holm is progressing. Coping work on masonry wall of the quay has been held up due to a lack of sand.

30 October 1941: Steam launch *Haslar* departed from Barry at 15.00 hours with rations for Steep Holm, which were successfully unloaded, but could not make Flat Holm as it was getting dark.

1 November 1941: Bristol Channel still closed to motor vessels, due to German mines. One steam boat is now the only craft in use for supplying the two islands. No materials have been taken over for a week Underwater telephone connection established with Flat Holm at 11.55 hours.

3 November 1941: Steam launch *Haslar*, towing motor boat *Peter Piper* without her engine running, has called at both islands.

5 November 1941: *Haslar* tows a barge to Flat Holm where a wireless message is received, from Steep Holm, reporting a casualty there needing to be picked up. Departure from Flat Holm at 19.00 hours, collection of casualty from Steep Holm, and return to Barry at 23.00 hours.

8 November 1941: Steam launch *Haslar* sails from Barry at 13.15 hours, this time towing Admiralty launch *Corrigoyle*, with rations for the islands.

9 November 1941: 930 Port Construction and Repair Company on Steep Holm help land underwater telephone cable from Brean Down.

13 November 1941: Reduction of Steep Holm detachment to 30 men of 930 Port Construction and Repair Company and 40 other ranks of the Pioneer Corps.

14 November 1941: Painting of the jetty on Flat Holm completed.

18 November 1941: Jetty decking on Steep Holm completed. Fendering is being fixed.

25 November 1941: Manpower and rations landed at Steep Holm for the first time in a week.

3 December 1941: Work starts on painting the newly completed jetty on Steep Holm.

5 December 1941: Boats sail to both islands but can land only at Steep Holm. The motor launch, which was being towed, struck a German mine and exploded near Flat Holm, a quarter of a mile offshore, with injuries to the engineer.

9 December 1941: Work commences on the jetty head extension at Flat Holm.

19 December 1941: Headquarters Fixed Defences Severn takes over the re-organised Cardiff Fire Command which now comprises Flat Holm Fire Command; Docks Fire Command (Cardiff); and Brean Down Fire Command. On Steep Holm, 189 Coast Battery, at Steep Holm North (Summit Basttery), has been transferred from 531 Regiment to the new 570 Regiment Royal Artillery.

21 December 1941: Telephone communication has been established between Steep Holm and the mainland.

24 December 1941: Major M. Thompson, the Officer Commanding 690 General Construction Company, arrives on Steep Holm to stay over Christmas. The boat carries three days' rations and Xmas fare.

26 December 1941: Return of Major Thompson from Steep Holm, with reports of an excellent Christmas dinner and appreciation from unit personnel and attachments. Reports from Flat Holm, however, are varied and indifferent.

3 January 1942: The detachment of one officer and 36 other ranks of 930 Port Construction and Repair Company on Steep Holm, plus their ten Pioneer Corps labourers, are attached to 690 General Construction Company of the Royal Engineers for rations and accommodation.

17 January 1942: Steep Holm South (Garden Battery) No.2 gun has been mounted, but is not yet ready for action.

30 January 1942: Steel for casting the beams of the Flat Holm low-water jetty was received at the beginning of the week and one beam has now been cast and is awaiting transfer to the island. Foundations for the masonry part of the jetty are all completed. Other work on improving the West Beach landing is continuing. On Steep Holm the masonry work on the low-water jetty continued until the tides prevented any further work. The base sections of the uprights for the extension to the pier-head quay are in position and scaffolding is being erected.

31 January 1942: Average distribution of personnel of 930 Port Construction and Repair Company during January — HQ Barry: 2 officers, 52 other ranks, and 10 Royal Artillery (attached). Steep Holm: 1 officer, 21 other ranks, and 10 Pioneer Corps (attached). Flat Holm: 1 officer, 16 other ranks. Strength of 570 Regiment, Royal

Artillery — 11 officers and 348 other ranks. 116 Pioneer Company — 4½ sections on Flat Holm and 3½ sections on Steep Holm.

7 February 1942: Thirty-five men of 188 Coast Battery, 570 Regiment Royal Artillery, have moved from Brean Down to their permanent station at Steep Holm South.

13 February 1942: Remainder of 188 Coast Battery arrive on Steep Holm.

17 March 1942: Second-Lieutenant Almond has crushed his toes in an accident on Steep Holm.

27 March 1942: Five Pioneer Corps men have been attached to 930 Port Construction and Repair Company on Flat Holm. One officer and 12 other ranks of the company are on the island.

1 April 1942: Strength of 570 Regiment, Royal Artillery — 16 officers and 360 other ranks. Work of mainland party of 116 Pioneer Company consists of loading steamers with stores and machinery for Flat Holm and Steep Holm. Island detachments engaged in digging and erecting gun sites, searchlight emplacements, living accommodation, ammunition stores, cable trenches, and unloading associated materials from steamers and barges.

7 April 1942: Bristol Channel Artillery operational as the Fixed Defences Severn, on a line from Lavernock Point in South Wales to Brean Down, Somerset, and placed under Western Command.

19 April 1942: The defences of Flat Holm and Steep Holm are inspected by the Prime Minister's son-in-law, Lieutenant-Colonel Duncan Sandys MP, the Financial

Secretary to the War Office, who had married Diana Churchill in 1935.

27 April 1942: Headquarters Fixed Defences Severn, having been moved from 12 James Street, Cardiff, is now operating from its new base at Swanbridge, near Penarth.

30 May 1942: Major H.G. Mason and Captain R.E. Wilson fly over Brean Down, during the afternoon, to observe the effectiveness of camouflage measures.

6 June 1942: Further flight, by Lieutenant Gold-Lewis of the Royal Artillery, for the purpose of observing and photographing the camouflage on Brean Down.

8 June 1942: C-section of 118 Light Aircraft Regiment in place on Flat Holm.

20 June 1942: Fixed Defences Severn now comprise —
1. Headquarters and Flat Holm Fire Command, of 570 Regiment Royal Artillery; 188 Coast Battery at Steep Holm North; 145 Coast Battery at Lavernock Point.
2. Docks Fire Command (Cardiff) with Headquarters 531 Regiment Royal Artillery; 130 Coast Battery at Nell's Point; 427 Coast Battery at Newport; and 430 Coast Battery at Cardiff.
3. Brean Down Fire Command — Headquarters 571 Regiment at Portishead with 365 Coast Battery stationed there, and 366 Coast Battery at Brean Down.

30 June 1942: Light Anti-Aircraft defences on Flat Holm (VP 510) operated by "A" Section of 365 Battery, Light Anti-Aicraft Regiment. Comprise Site 1 at T661864 with one Light Machine Gun and two 40-mm Bofors guns. Site 2 at T664861 with one L.M.G. and one Bofors. Site 3 at

T661864 with three L.M.G. Site 4 at T664861 with three L.M.G.

1 July 1942: One section of 116 Pioneer Company withdrawn from Steep Holm to Wenvoe Camp.

2 July 1942: Three sections of 116 Pioneer Company withdrawn from Steep Holm and four sections from Flat Holm, returning to Wenvoe Camp.

3 July 1942: 184 Coast Battery have arrived from East Blockhouse to man Flat Holm North and have relieved 189 Battery. Both batteries are attached to 570 Regiment, Royal Artillery.

4 July 1942: Detachments of 930 Port Construction and Repair Company, Royal Engineers, withdrawn from Steep Holm and Flat Holm, with their work handed over to 690 General Construction Company. 930 Company remaining island manpower now as follows. Flat Holm jetty construction — one officer, 16 other ranks, and five Pioneer Company (attached). Steep Holm jetty construction — one non-commissioned officer, ten other ranks, and six Pioneer Company (attached).

7 July 1942: Major H.G. Mason of 571 Regiment Royal Artillery attends an investiture at Buckingham Palace to receive the MBE decoration.

3 August 1942: Title of 690 General Construction Company changed to 690 Artisan Works Company, Royal Engineers.

5 August 1942: 01.42 hours. Red alert at Cardiff. Site J16, operated by 351 Heavy Anti-Aircraft Battery on Flat Holm, fires 27 rounds at enemy aircraft. No effect.

6 August 1942: 600 rounds of S.A.P. 4.5-inch ammunition delivered to 351 Heavy Anti-Aircraft Battery on Flat Holm. Holding now 800 rounds.

8 August 1942: Major M.W. McDonald RA posted to command 571 Regiment as Major H.G. Mason MBE, RA leaves to command 561 Regiment. No.2 gun on Flat Holm out of action.

9 August 1942: 351 Heavy Anti-Aircraft Battery on Flat Holm carry out and anti-tank shoot, with the target being three empty petrol cans towed behind a single Hong Kong float.

10 August 1942: Heavy rains and fresh winds prevent a boat reaching Flat Holm with mechanical assistance to repair No.2 gun which is still out of action.

12 August 1942: Royal Army Ordnance Corps personnel taken to Flat Holm for gun repairs.

13 August 1942: Advanced party of 719 Artisan Works Company, Royal Engineers, has left Barry Docks on the duty boat for "Bristol Channel Islands Site XF" (Steep Holm).

24 August 1942: Light Anti-Aircraft sites on Flat Holm now listed as Site 1 at T660864, Site 2 at T664863, and Site 3 at T662862.

26 August 1942: Practice shoot after dark from 366 Coast Battery at Brean Down, while cinema entertainment is provided during the evening on Flat Holm.

28 August 1942: Headquarters 719 Artisan Works Company being moved to Penarth to replace 690 Artisan

Works Company, Royal Engineers. They are to work on coast defence installation and accommodation on Flat Holm and Steep Holm.

29 August 1942: No.1 and 2 sections of 719 Artisan Works Company crossed by boat at 06.00 hours to "Bristol Channel Islands Site XD" — the island of Flat Holm.

2 September 1942: Brigadier Coast Artillery and Colonel Ferard visit 351 Heavy Anti-Aircraft Battery on Flat Holm for a practice shoot. Sixteen rounds fired.

14 September 1942: Searchlights renumbered. The Flat Holm searchlight is now known as Fire Command 051 and is operated by 307 Battery, 37 Searchlight Regiment.

22 October 1942: Stormy weather. No duty boat sailed to Flat Holm but steamship *Hasler* endeavoured to put a boat ashore. This was holed in the attempt but managed to return to *Hasler* without further incident.

23 October 1942: Sea conditions continue to be very rough. Another accident, to the launch proceeding to Flat Holm, necessitates the Battery Commander, 351 Heavy Anti-Aircraft Battery, and party staying the night on the mainland.

31 October 1942: Entertainments National Service Association visit to the islands starts with an evening concert on Steep Holm, featuring the Fowler Brothers, Isobel, Anne and Elsie.

1 November 1942: Concert in the evening on Flat Holm.

5 November 1942: Cinema show in the evening on Flat Holm.

12 November 1942: Death of a gunner, of 531 Regiment, on Steep Holm.

17 November 1942: Two 4.5-inch guns on Flat Holm taken over by 205 Coast Battery, Royal Artillery. 26 other ranks from 351 Heavy Anti-Aircraft Regiment have returned to Lavernock Fort.

20 November 1942: Brigade I.F.C. visit Flat Holm.

21 November 1942: Amputated 2A Predictor delivered to Flat Holm and installed in the North Battery. Though dropped twice in transit by the Royal Army Ordnance Corps it is working perfectly.

4 December 1942: Second Amputated Predictor received on Flat Holm, for use in the South Battery, but some difficulty is being experienced with the Q.E. dials.

7 December 1942: 188 Coast Battery at Steep Holm South and 189 Coast Battery at Steep Holm North, formerly with 570 Regiment, have been regimented with 571 Regiment Royal Artillery. 146 Coast Battery has ceased to be regimented with 559 Regiment, and has been re-regimented with 570 Regiment for deployment at Flat Holm South. 205 Coast Battery, manning Flat Holm North, has ceased to be an independent unit and has also been regimented with 570 Regiment Royal Artillery.

8 December 1942: Personnel of 146 Coast Battery take over Height and Range finding at Flat Holm South from 351 Heavy Anti-Aircraft Battery.

12 December 1942: Colonel King visits Flat Holm.

13 December 1942: Special boat sent to Flat Holm to pick up an injured man.

17 December 1942: Day shoots by 366 Coast Battery, seaward from Brean Down, and 189 Coast Battery from Steep Holm North. Their firing continued into the night. Also seaward night shoot practice by 188 Coast Battery from Steep Holm South.

24 December 1942: Christmas Eve cinema show on Flat Holm.

26 December 1942: Boxing Day concert on Flat Holm described as very good.

29 December 1942: Officer of the Royal Electrical and Mechanical Engineers visits Flat Holm to inspect the 40 mm Bofors equipment.

31 December 1942: Flat Holm North site became operational during the month.

2 January 1943: Stores and equipment handed over by 351 Heavy Anti-Aircraft Battery on Flat Holm to 205 Coast Battery of 570 Coast Regiment, Royal Artillery.

7 January 1943: Predictors on Flat Holm both out of action and replaced by Unamputated Predictors. North Battery currently not operational pending arrival of No.7 cable.

10 January 1943: R.M.O carries out aircraft calibration of gun laying on Flat Holm.

11 January 1943: Four Light Anti-Aircraft sites listed on Flat Holm. Site 1 at T660864. Site 2 at T664861. Site 3 at T664863. Site 4 at T664862. All operated by "B" section

440 Battery, 127 Light Anti-Aircraft Regiment. The Heavy Anti-Aircraft on Flat Holm is at T663863 and operated by three sections of 351 Heavy Anti-Aircraft Battery.

15 January 1943: Air Co-Operation exercise carried out on Flat Holm.

18 January 1943: 440 Battery of 127 Light Anti-Aircraft Regiment replaced on Flat Holm by "C" section 306 Coast Battery, 98 Regiment Royal Artillery.

20 January 1943: 366 Coast Battery of 571 Regiment has completed interchange of stations with 189 Coast Battery at Steep Holm North. the latter are now at Brean Down.

21 January 1943: Practice seaward by 205 Coast Battery from Flat Holm North. Full charge of 4.5-inch fired in dual role at set range.

1 February 1943: 570 Regiment has taken over the heavy anti-aircraft commitments of 146 Coast Battery at Flat Holm South and 205 Coast Battery at Flat Holm North. Equipment four 4.5-inch dual role guns. Movement of personnel of 351 Heavy Anti-Aircraft Battery from Flat Holm has been temporarily delayed.

2 February 1943: Flat Holm has been vacated by personnel of 351 Heavy Anti-Aircraft Battery who are proceeding to Newport, Cardiff, and Caerwent.

13 February 1943: Practice seaward by 295 Coast Battery from Flat Holm North; three series.

16 February 1943: Two German aircraft engaged by the Flat Holm batteries. Eight rounds fired but no result.

12 March 1943: 189 Coast Battery return to Steep Holm from Brean Down and relieve 188 Coast Battery at Steep Holm South. 15.30 hours — practice shoot by 205 Coast Battery at Flat Holm North; three rounds fired.

13 March 1943: German Focke-Wulf FW 190 engaged at 7,800 feet by the 4.5-inch guns on Flat Holm. This is their extreme range and there was no result.

17 March 1943: Steep Holm South, the double 6-inch naval gun emplacements at Garden Battery, have been handed by 189 Coast Battery to Care and Maintenance. Initial caretaker party of 12 men to be reduced shortly.

23 April 1943: Seven rounds fired at an enemy aircraft engaged by 205 Coast Battery from Flat Holm North. No results.

6 May 1943: 10.45 hours — seaward practice of two series by 146 Coast Battery from Flat Holm South. 11.30 hours — seaward practice by 205 Coast Battery from Flat Holm North; one series.

18 May 1943: 02.52 hours — Flat Holm batteries open fire on enemy aircraft at 4,800 to 9,200 feet, in an engagement that lasts 35 minutes. 205 Coast Battery fired 108 rounds from Flat Holm North and 146 Coast Battery, at Flat Holm South, fired 86 rounds.

20 May 1943: The 4.5-inch dual role batteries on Flat Holm practise their firing at air targets. A total of 76 rounds fired from Flat Holm North and 55 rounds from Flat Holm South.

27 May 1943: Interchange of 188 Coast Battery, now at Steep Holm North, and 366 Coast Battery, who have returned to Brean Down.

24 June 1943: 20.00 hours — practice seaward by both Flat Holm batteries, firing two series each.

10 July 1943: Practice seaward at 10.00 hours by both Flat Holm batteries. Searchlight practice at 23.00 hours by 146 and 205 Coast Batteries on Flat Holm and 145 Coast Battery of 170 Regiment at Lavernock.

23 July 1943: 03.28 hours — single enemy aircraft engaged by 205 Coast Battery at Flat Holm North, firing six rounds, and by 145 Coast Battery at Flat Holm South, with four rounds. No results.

26 July 1943: Practice firing seaward at 10.00 hours by 146 Coast Battery from Flat Holm South.

28 July 1943: 15.00 hours — anti-aircraft practice by 205 Coast Battery from Flat Holm North, firing six rounds.

31 July 1943: 01.40 hours — single enemy aircraft engaged by 205 Coast Battery at Flat Holm North and by 146 Coast Battery at Flat Holm South, firing 16 rounds each. No results.

16 August 1943: Lieutenant-Colonel R.A. King assumes command of the Fixed Defences Severn, on the posting of Colonel C.L. Ferard MC to Fixed Defences Forth.

13 September 1943: 21.30 hours — searchlight practice by the two batteries on Flat Holm and the mainland lights at Lavernock.

View of Castle Rock from East Beach,
Flat Holm Local Nature Reserve,
South Glamorgan County Council.

SL-226

*Reproduced by kind permission of the artist
Mr Ley Kenyon D.F.C & produced for The Flat Holm
Trading Co. Ltd by Michael J. Allen (0202) 743953.
Printed by Dolphin Printers (Poole) Dorset*

POST CARD

POST CARD

Lesser Black-backed gull *Larus fuscus*
on West Beach,
Flat Holm Local Nature Reserve,
South Glamorgan.
Photo: Ann Benn ARPS

Flat Holm Project, Pierhead, Barry Docks, Barry, South Glamorgan, Wales. CF62 5QS Tel. (01446) 747661
Printed by J. Arthur Dixon

FLAT HOLM LOCAL NATURE RESERVE
South Glamorgan County Council

SL-94

POST CARD

Produced for the Flat Holm Society by
Delpool Ltd. (0202) 743953. Original water colour by
D Mayne Stephens of Dinas Powis, South Glamorgan.
Printed by Dolphin Printers (Poole) Dorset.

20 September 1943: Gun practice seaward at 10.00 hours by 187 Coast Battery from Newport. Searchlight practice at 21.30 hours by the batteries at Lavernock and Flat Holm.

29 September 1943: Three-pounder sub-calibre shoot by 188 Coast Battery of 571 Regiment from Steep Holm North during the day is followed by 6-inch seaward practice at night.

20 October 1943: "Flood Tide" is implemented by Western Command and redundant fortifications are stood-down. In Fixed Defences Severn the emplacements at Lavernock (145 Coast Battery), Brean Down (366 Coast Battery), and Steep Holm North (188 Coast Battery) have ceased to have an operational role. All three have been reduced to Care and Maintenance status.

29 October 1943: Seaward practice by 366 Coast Battery, using 75-mm weapons, will probably be its last operational shots of this war.

1 November 1943: 571 Regiment Royal Artillery, with units on Steep Holm and Brean Down, has ceased to be operational. Its officer and six other ranks at Portishead, in 184 Coast Battery, have been placed under a Home Guard (Mixed) Battery.

18 November 1943: 11.00 hours — practice seaward by 205 Coast Battery from Flat Holm North; two series. 12.00 hours — practice seaward by 146 Coast Battery from Flat Holm South; also two series.

20 November 1943: 11.00 hours — practice seaward from Flat Holm North; one series.

26 November 1943: 13.45 hours — practice seaward from Flat Holm South, followed at 14.45 hours by similar firings from Flat Holm North; both two series.

10 February 1944: Seaward practice at 21 hours from Flat Holm South and North; two series each.

11 February 1944: Seaward practice at 11.30 hours by both Flat Holm batteries; four series each.

20 February 1944: Headquarters Fixed Defences Severn are re-located. Closed at Swanbridge, and re-opened at Nell's Point, Barry Island. 570 Regiment headquarters also moved there, from Craiglands in Redbrink Close, Barry Island.

22 February 1944: Practice seaward by 146 Coast Battery from Flat Holm North; one series.

23 February 1944: Practice seaward by 146 Coast Battery from Flat Holm South and 205 Coast Battery from Flat Holm North; three series.

29 February 1944: The strength of 570 Regiment is currently 20 officers and 434 other ranks.

27-28 March 1944: 23.41 to 00.11 hours — enemy aircraft engaged by 146 Coast Battery from Flat Holm South and 205 Coast Battery from Flat Holm North. Six targets approaching from south to north and south-west to north-east, between 12,600 and 28,000 feet. Speed from 300 to 350 mph. A total of 109 rounds were fired but with no result.

1 April 1944: Orders issued for the disbanding of the Headquarters Fixed Defences Severn. 184 Coast Battery

(Portishead), and Care and Maintenance parties of 188 Coast Battery (Brean Down), 189 Coast Battery (Steep Holm South), and 366 Coast Battery (Steep Holm North) to be re-regimented from 571 Regiment to 570 Regiment Royal Artillery. Composition of the reorganised 570 Regiment to be Headquarters (Barry Island); 205 Coast Battery (Flat Holm North); 146 Coast Battery (Flat Holm South); 430 Coast Battery (Cardiff); 187 Coast Battery (Newport); 184 Coast Battery (Portishead); 188 Coast Battery (Brean Down); 366 Coast Battery (Steep Holm North); 189 Coast Battery (Steep Holm South); 145 Coast Battery (Lavernock); and 170 Coast Battery (Nell's Point).

8 April 1944: C.A. No.1 Mark V brought into operation on Flat Holm.

20 April 1944: Disbandment completed of Headquarters Fixed Defences Severn. 14.15 hours — launch 1513 from the R.A.F.'s No 45 Air Sea Rescue and Marine Craft Unit at Barry called to assist War Department vessel *Princessa* in difficulties off Flat Holm.

28 April 1944: Gun Laying Mark III radar apparatus, for anti-aircraft use, arrived on Flat Holm.

15 May 1944: Two enemy aircraft engaged for 15 minutes by 146 Coast Battery from Flat Holm South and 205 Coast Battery at Flat Holm North. No results claimed.

25 May 1944: R.A.F. Air Sea Rescue launch ST 1513 from Barry again called out to assist War Department vessel *Princessa*, drifting near Flat Holm. The launch stood by until the vessel was taken in tow by the tug *Blazer*.

31 May 1944: Strength of 570 Regiment currently 22 officers and 509 other ranks.

4 June 1944: Severn Fire Command begins a month of practice firings, seaward, by all operational batteries of 570 Regiment.

19 July 1944: Fixed Defences Severn now comprise Z Works — Flat Holm North Battery with two 4.5-inch Coast Artillery and Anti-Aircraft dual role guns, and two C.A.S.L.s (M). Y Works — Flat Holm South Battery with ditto weapons systems. X Works — Cardiff with two 75-mm Q.F. and five C.A.S.L.s (2M and 3 F). Additionally, in Care and Maintenance with two storekeepers at each, there are a further two pairs of 6-inch guns at each of the following batteries: Lavernock, Nell's Point, Brean Down, Steep Holm North, and Steep Holm South.

24 July 1944: Radar trials on Flat Holm.

2 August 1944: A further month of seaward practice firings begins, involving all operational batteries of 570 Regiment.

2 October 1944: Practice firings, continuing until 22 October, by both batteries on Flat Holm and those at Portishead and Cardiff.

5 December 1944: Practice firings seaward by 146 Coast Battery at Flat Holm South and 205 Coast Battery at Flat Holm North.

7 December 1944: More practice firings by both batteries on Flat Holm, effectively using up surplus ammunition.

18 December 1944: Both batteries on Flat Holm become non-operational.

30 April 1945: Strength of 570 Regiment now reduced to 11 officers and 204 other ranks.

12 June 1945: Orders issued for the disbanding of 570 Regiment.

22 June 1945: Disbandment of 570 Regiment completed.

Principal Sources

WO 166/2065: Cardiff Fixed Defences
War Diary 1940-41
WO 166/7287: Severn Fixed Defences
War Diary 1942
WO 166/11261: Severn Fixed Defences
War Diary 1943
WO 166/14955: Severn Fxed Defences
War Diary 1944
WO 166/1733: 531 Coast Regiment
War Diary 1941
WO 166/7153: 531 Coast Regiment
War Diary 1942
WO 166/7187: 570 Coast Regiment
War Diary 1942
WO 166/11463: 570 Coast Regiment
War Diary 1943
WO 166/15051: 570 Coast Regiment
War Diary 1944
WO 166/16867: 570 Coast Regiment
War Diary 1945
WO 166/7188: 571 Coast Regiment
War Diary 1942
WO 166/11464: 571 Coast Regiment
War Diary 1943
WO 166/15052: 571 Coast Regiment
War Diary 1944
WO 166/1769: 130 Coast Battery
War Diary 1941
WO 166/7191: 130 Coast Battery
War Diary 1942
WO 166/1774: 145 Coast Battery
War Diary 1940-41
WO 166/7195: 170 Coast Battery
War Diary 1942
WO 166/7566: 351 H.A.A. Battery
War Diary 1942
WO 166/11676: 351 H.A.A. Battery
War Diary 1943
WO 166/1842: 365 Coast Battery
War Diary 1940-41
WO 166/1843: 366 Coast Battery
War Diary 1941

WO 166/3547: Glamorgan Fortress Coy.
War Diary 1939-40
WO 166/3570: 29 (Railway) Survey Coy.
War Diary 1940-41
WO 166/5600: 116 Pioneer Coy.
War Diary 1940-41
WO 166/10008: 116 Pioneer Coy. War
Diary 1942
WO 166/3937: 930 Port Construction &
Repair Coy. War Diary 1941
WO 166/8348: 930 Port Construction &
Repair Coy. War Diary 1942
WO 166/3874: 690 General Construction
Coy. War Diary 1941
WO 166/8290: 690 General Construction
Coy. War Diary 1942
WO 166/8315: 719 General Construction
Coy. War Diary 1942
WO 166/12240: 719 General Construction
Coy. War Diary 1943
WO 166/2286: 45 A.A. Brigade
War Diary 1941
WO 166/7402: 45 A.A. Brigade
War Diary 1942
WO 166/11219: 45 A.A. Brigade
War Diary 1943
WO 192/155: Flat Holm Fort Record Book
1939-45
WO 199/1638: Coastal Defences (Southern
Command) 1940-42
WO 199/1639: Coastal Defences (Southern
Command) 1942-43
WO 199/1640: Coastal Defences (Southern
Command) 1943
AIR 29/448: No. 45 Air Sea Rescue Unit
R.A.F. (O.R.B.) 1942-46
Lineage Book of British Land Forces
1660-1975 Vol. 2 (1984)

WARTIME MEMORIES OF FLAT HOLM

by David Benger

At the beginning of 1941 I was a second lieutenant, serving in Coast Artillery on the sea-forts at Portland Harbour, where we had just survived the excitements of the Battle of Britain. In May of that year I was posted to the 72nd Coast Training Regiment, RA, Norton Camp, Yarmouth, Isle of Wight (c/o Lt.Col Patchell). In peacetime this camp had been the Savoy Holiday Camp. There we trained new Coast Artillery Batteries. I left in August 1941 with the newly-formed 188 Coast Battery (Capt. Maunder). This, and 189 Coast Battery, formed at the same time, were destined to man the six-inch naval guns on Steep Holm. On arrival at Barry Island we were attached to 570 Coast Regiment RA (c/o Lt.Col Ben Bolt) and accommodated at Nell's Point Battery, now a holiday camp.

My first landing on Flat Holm was a week or two later, when I was detailed to take pay out to the men working on the island. We travelled on a filthy old coastal steamer laden with building materials, and the crew and ship strongly reminded me of the film *The Maggie*, about a Clyde Puffer. By a display of inept seamanship we managed to ram the jetty on arrival, an entertainment much enjoyed by the troops. No guns were yet emplaced, but the Royal Engineers had the North Battery, Nissen huts, water tower, latrines, magazines searchlight emplacements etc. well under construction, and the Victorian barrack rooms and hospital under repair. The farmhouse had been made into an officers' mess.

Within a few days I was sent off on a series of courses at the Coast Artillery School, Llandudno, and the Western Command Weapon Training School, Altcar, Liverpool. By the time these were over we were into November, and the Battery had moved to Brean Down, Somerset, where it was navvying, helping to build the six-inch Naval gun battery which would become part of 571 Coast Regiment. Steep Holm was still not ready for occupation. I was shortly posted to Iceland, where I arrived at the beginning of December.

Within a few days Pearl Harbour had taken place, the Americans were in the war, and preparations were made for the U.S. to take complete responsibility for Iceland. As a matter of fact, a large force of U.S. Marines was unofficially already there, some sharing our camp. We returned to the U.K. in May 1942. My Battery was posted first to mid-Wales, then to Milford Haven, and finally to Barry, much to my surprise. We were immediately shipped out to Flat Holm for navvying, where much progress had been made since I had last seen it. I was almost immediately detached from my Battery and sent to the HQ of Commander, Fixed Defences, Severn (Col. Cecil Ferard) as an extra staff officer. He rapidly discovered my love of model-making and got me on to building training devices. I did not attach much importance to this at the time, but afterwards realised that I was being tested out as a future Battery Commander. This attachment finished when my Battery was posted to 571 Coast Regiment to take over the guns (six-inch Naval) at Battery Point, Portishead.

About September I was posted back to Flat Holm (570 Coastal Regiment), now commanded by Lt.Col. Rex King RA, without any particular reason being given. There I found that all the guns were emplaced and in action, the North Battery's buildings being complete, South Battery (Lighthouse) not being started. At South Battery the predictor and guns were in sandbag emplacements, the Barr and Stroud Height/Rangefinder was on a mobile trolley without any defence at all, and the Command Post was a flimsy half-Nissen hut. The guns were manned by 351 Heavy A.A. Battery (Major Lovell).

The reason for my posting now started to become clearer. The original idea had been that the guns would be manned by an A.A. Battery, but that the primary role would be anti-ship, and thus tactical and administrative control would be by Coast Artillery. A.A. Command and the Battery concerned were resisting this idea. The officers and men concerned had probably realised that their avenues of promotion would be considerably decreased if they were cut off from the enormous and growing field of A.A. Command. Moreover, the H.A.A. officers and men showed an entire indifference to learning how to engage enemy ships. Here a new solution was being looked at. If H.A.A. would not learn to fire at ships, Coast Artillery would have to learn to fire at aircraft.

About this time 205 Coast Battery arrived on the island, having just returned from the Faeroe Islands. Lieut. Denis Horder (of 205) and I were sent together on a course at the 3rd A.A. Group School, Porthcawl, to learn everything about anti-aircraft gunnery. We returned to Flat Holm in November, and found that Horder was to command North Battery while I would have South. 351 H.A.A. Battery helped with training the Coast Artillery gunners in the new discipline.

Unfortunately my Battery (146 Coast Battery) had been made up by cadres from a large number of units in Western Command, and all had taken advantage of the opportunity to get rid of their ne'er-do-wells and military misfits. My first sight of my office showed a trestle table piled high with army crime sheets listing all their horrible offences. This was an impossible start, and within a few days they were all on their way back to their units, accompanied by orders from Western Command to send some proper soldiers. Now we were in business. In the reshuffle I was delighted to pick up some of my old stalwarts from Iceland days, rugged Territorials from the Harwich area, of whom I could be absolutely sure.

By now the Sappers had gone, and we were on our own. 205 Battery and 146 Battery were quickly trained up to standard, and 351 H.A.A. Battery withdrew. 205 Battery was able to work to a normal routine, but 146 set about building proper gun positions, using the skills of gunners who had been in the building industry. We had to make some deep excavations in solid rock with pneumatic drills. The positions were built in hollow concrete blocks, unlike North Battery, which had been built in solid concrete. Simultaneously we had to continue gunnery training, so we worked hard. Saturday afternoon and Sunday afternoon were the only times off. When the gun platforms were complete we started on excavating the site for the Command Post, using the spoil to fill part of the moat and provide a path linking the Command Post and guns. We made such good progress that Western Command looked favourably on our efforts and finished the Command Post for us with civilian labour, who also built the island hospital.

At first both Batteries were Captain's commands, but they were later upgraded to Major's commands. Normally, I would think, Horder and I would have been too young to qualify for this rank, as we were both only 27, but as the Batteries were dual-role Coast and A.A., nobody but ourselves had the required experience. Each Battery had four subalterns and about 150 NCOs and men. The Batteries shared a GLII and a GLIII radar. GLIIIs were rare at this time, and Flat Holm was given one because it was an excellent site, free from unwanted spurious echoes.

Each Battery had two 4.5 inch Static H.A.A. guns connected by Magslip transmission to its predictor (Sperry No. 2A), at the Command Post. The guns had been specially modified to be allowed to be depressed enough to engage ships. This slightly reduced their maximum elevation. Each Battery also had at the Command Post a combined Height/Range Finder and a plotting room. A

Coast Artillery Observation Post was built on to the front of the Command Post.

The 4.5 inch A.A. Gun was designed purely for A.A. purposes and was poorly adapted for shooting at ships. The gunlayers had no direct sights, i.e., could not see the target. They laid the gun by matching pointers on dials from information transmitted by the predictor. The predictor also was badly designed for anti-ship purposes, requiring a base of thousands of feet to be set into it to give accurate data. For anti-ship purposes this base would have been only the differential height of ship and predictor, a few feet, so completely diferent procedures were needed. Instead of allowing the predictor to work out the range, we set the range in from the optical rangefinder, and adjusted fire by observation.

How it would have worked out against an enemy moving fast and "jinking" we never found out. But there is no doubt that had not the invention of the jet aircraft overnight made all conventional guns obsolete, in the post-war period the Flat Holm dual role prototype would have become general for coast defence, and a suitable dual purpose gun would have evolved.

There were frequent air raid alerts and engagements of one or two German bombers on "nuisance" raids, though there were one or two more intense blitzes on Cardiff. The Flat Holm site was found to be important because for one reason or another its radars often managed to be the first to pick up incoming hostile aircraft in the Cardiff gun-defended area and to put all the other radars on target. It was apparent from plotter traces that enemy pilots often flew over Steep Holm and Flat Holm and maintained this course to find the eastern edge of Cardiff. From time to time a rocket-barrage was fired over Flat Holm to try to catch these intruders out at this practice. This never worked, but it made life interesting for us underneath as all the refuse from the rockets rained down on our heads. No doubt it was done with the kindest of intentions.

Discipline was not a problem on the island itself, but there was a considerable problem of men overstaying leave. This was usually dealt with by fines. "Confined to barracks" meant nothing, as we all were, all the time. Leave for officers and men alike was, in a three-month cycle, seven days, 24 hours, 48 hours, 24 hours. We were allowed to leave on the duty boat the previous day and return the day following the end of our leave. Sport on the island was limited by the terrain, but British soldiers will play football anywhere, as ours did. Swimming was strictly forbidden, hence we never lost a man. Many turned to making toys for their children from scraps of timber. There was a small library, housed in what was once the isolation hospital laundry. The isolation hospital's two large wards were turned into a NAAFI canteen and a cinema and concert hall, with real curtains supplied by ENSA. We built the stage from timber from packing cases which had protected American aircraft unloaded as deck cargoes from ships arriving in Barry Docks. We got a film about once a fortnight, and occasionally a concert party came out and gave us a show.

In addition to the two A.A. guns per battery, we each had a Bofors light A.A. gun (manned by the battery office staff) and a Bren gun on an A.A. tripod. We had frequent practice shoots against sea and air towed targets, and the searchlights were similarly practised against fast motor-launches. One weapon we were glad to see the back of was the ex-Royal Navy two-inch U.P. (unrotating projectile) projector. This was like a large pillar box with wings stuffed with rockets, for use against dive-bombers. The rockets were highly erratic in performance, and we were glad to be allowed to fire off the ammunition, with many excitements, and get rid of them.

We were not totally alone on the island. The farmer, Mr Harris (mentioned by other contributors), lived in a small cottage near the farmhouse and grazed a few sheep, who cropped the grass down to a delightful springy sward. It was said that the Post Office paid Mr Harris ten shillings a week for acting as island postman and delivering letters — to himself. Three Trinity House keepers manned the foghorn and maintained the light, though the light was never lit throughout the war. We got on well with all these people, who through us enjoyed the benefit of regular mail and papers, and the use of the NAAFI canteen and a welcome at whatever entertainment was going.

We were very much a self-sufficient community, apart from food and water coming from the mainland. Anything that went wrong we had to mend ourselves. The island was a healthy place, and the MO and his small hospital had very little to do. The island was a favourite place to visit for "Top Brass" from Western Command and elsewhere, and had to be kept neat and tidy at all times. Our CO (Lt. Col. Rex King) was a hospitable man who loved showing his command off to visitors. These tours followed a set pattern — special launch, reception at the jetty by Battery Commander, walk round the island with explanations, drinks in the mess, lunch, more drinks, and final departure, with sighs of relief from the residents. In practice the officers on the island were very abstemious, never knowing by day or night when the air raid alarm would sound, and never off duty.

One thing that always interested visitors was the way we wasted nothing. The swill was used to fatten our very fine collection of pigs, who were regularly sent to market, at Cowbridge I believe, and got good prices. The garden behind the farmhouse was brought back into cultivation by one of the batmen (Gunner Wyatt, one of the stalwarts from Iceland), and provided plenty of fresh vegetables. We also kept chickens and had plenty of new laid eggs. I think we must have been the original defenders of the ecology.

Flat Holm was not a paradise, and some of the men probably hated it, but we tried to make it as tolerable as possible, and there was a great feeling of comradeship and the minimum of "military nonsense". I remember my time there with pleasure and affection, and in recent years, while living in Penarth close by, it was good to be able to help a little in preserving the history of the island.

A few days after D-Day the Batteries were "stood down", and I was immediately posted elsewhere. Most of the officers and men were formed into a Royal Artillery Infantry Unit, whose last act in the war was to take the surrender of the Channel Islands when the war in Europe was over.

A NIGHT ON FLAT HOLM, WINTER 1943

by David Benger

I lie asleep on an uncomfortable camp-bed, to which I have long become immured, in a sparsely-furnished bedroom in the old farmhouse on Flat Holm. My only luxury is some blackout curtains, made from the usual miserable black cotton. My wife has machined them up for me during a leave, and added some coloured ribbon across the bottom to cheer them up. A rickety chair and a home-made table compete the furniture. Nobody sleeps deeply, and everyone has his clothes piled where they can instantly be found in the dark.

We have spent our usual winter evening, dinner, a pint of beer, and a few hands of Pontoon in the draughty ante-room where when gales blow we have to put down hollow concrete blocks in strategic positions to keep the lino firmly on the floor. This evening we have had the bonus of Tommy Handley's "ITMA" on the radio to cheer us up. After an hour's noisy play, nobody has won or lost more than the cost of 20 Players cigarettes, then about 7½p. We are lucky to have this radio, for the island lighting generator produces direct current, and ordinary sets will not do. We have scoured Cardiff for similar sets for the men's barrack rooms, and most now have them.

At ten o'clock, from the old muzzle-loader emplacement fifty yards away, we hear the roar of the generator falter and fail, and the lights go out: even the Royal Engineers must sleep some time. Now we have only the light of the wide coal grate. A young officer trying to finish his letter to his wife in time for tomorrow's boat groans with irritation. It is a familiar sound. Now by the light of a hurricane lamp and torches we clean our teeth and make our way to bed. The island is quite still now, apart from a murmur of wind and the unending roar of the sea. I look out of the bedroom window and see that apart from a few well-defined clouds, the sky is quite bright. It is Bombers' Moon.

All preparations have been made. In the Command Posts of both batteries two officers, and predictor and plotter teams are ready, with telephonists and lookouts at their posts. Gun detachments are in huts close by. We have four minutes in which to be ready if there is an alarm.

At one a.m. the expected happens. We are woken by the wail of the siren mounted on the roof of south battery Command Post (the bracket is still there fifty years later). No time for military formality. I pull on trousers, battle-dress blouse and an old pair of flying boots which require no lacing, seize a steel helmet and run. Other indistinguishable forms too are racing across the island, stumbling against hammocks. Rabbits and sheep scurry away into the darkness, more scared of us than any enemy bomber. Over on the left in the centre of the island I hear the sound of the radar diesel generator being hand-cranked — no luxurious self-starters in those days. It is near freezing, the oil is thick and cold, and it is taking two blaspheming gunners to turn it, even at half-compression. As I listen, it bursts uncertainly into life, and settles down into a disciplined roar as the governor takes charge. This is the most welcome sound I can hope for, for on the functioning of this engine depend both radars and all the instruments which will direct the guns. We reach the floor of the Command Post, dodging an onrush of gunners, boots still unlaced, clumping towards the guns. The team is already round the Sperry Predictor, its instrument lights glowing in the darkness. Down in the Plotting Room another team has taken post, and the telephonist already has the headset of the line to Gun Operations Room buttoned round his neck. We report ready for action, just within four minutes.

Down at the guns, the muzzle-covers are off, the breeches open for the first round, which already stands by the fuse setter. Automatic loading is needed, for the time from setting the fuse to firing the gun must be no more than ten seconds. Now all we need is a target.

Far to the south, probably over Portland, RAF radar has picked up a hostile aircraft heading on a course for Bristol and Cardiff. All radars in the Gun Defended Area are now searching the skies above Somerset for the first faint blip on their screens. Suddenly, and not for the first time, it is Flat Holm's GLII which picks up the first blip, and at once all radars in the area seach the same spot. G.O.R. gives the order to engage. Information flows from radar to plotter to predictor to gun, and the first rounds crash out into the darkness. Simultaneously the North Battery opens up. There is little to see, for we are using flashless propellant, but the noise is deafening. The gun detachments work in darkness and silence, their routine perfected by countless hours of drill.

After ten minutes the target has disappeared from radar screens as suddenly as it appeared. It seems to have dropped no bombs, and possibly was no more than a nuisance intruder, getting the sirens going and interfering with the war effort in night shifts. The All Clear is not given for another hour. The gunners tidy away spent cartridge cases, and are sent into the shelter on the gun-floor for a smoke. Finally comes the order to stand down, and simultaneously through the darkness comes a clank of buckets. The battery sergeant major, bless him, has turned out one of the cooks to get some tea going, and arrives with two loaded gunners. What has not been slopped over en route is distributed. By a sensible Army tradition, the men are served first, so that if anybody goes without it will be the officers, who will be in the best possible position to get something done about it.

As I drink my mug of this fearful brew (too much tea, too much Ideal milk, too much sugar) I ponder the night with relief. Always on this site there is the worry that No 1 gun is going to forget the proximity of the Trinity House buildings, and I do not wish to be remembered throughout the Royal Artillery as the first Battery Commander to shoot down a friendly lighthouse. No 2 gun can't — we have built a sort of gallows to protect the barrel from straying into that arc of fire.

The men are dismissed. Tomorrow will be busy, for not only will they have extra maintenance to do on the guns, but there will be ammunition to bring up from the magazines to replace what we have fired. The gun-barrels will have to be scrubbed out with boiling water to release the corrosive fumes of cordite, then they will have to be dried out and oiled. In the Royal Artillery, a neglected gun is the biggest crime in the calendar, indeed something unimaginable.

We make our way back to our beds to get what sleep we can, and hand the island back to the sheep and rabbits. Soon it will be dawn, another day, and perhaps the same sort of night. There have been many such, and there will be many more.

FIRST WIRELESS MESSAGES

The first wireless messages ever transmitted across water were made during May 1897 by Guglielmo Marconi and his assistant George Kemp. The diary of Mr Kemp provides the details of these events.

<u>Thursday 6 May 1897</u>

Left Paddington for Cardiff and then on to Lavernock to see the mast and found that a long cable had been fixed which stretched out beyond low water mark for the purpose of earth connection.

<u>Friday 7 May</u>

I packed Mr Marconi's transmitter into a small tug at 6.30 a.m., together with the transmitting and receiving apparatus belonging to the Parallel Wire system of Mr W.H. Preece CB., FRS. Prepared Mr Marconi's transmitter in a small hut close to the mast, and slept at a small house owned by the person in charge of the Cremation House [of the Isolation Hospital].

<u>Saturday 8 May</u>

Transmitter working but I was not satisfied with the insulation of the cylinder and stays.

<u>Sunday 9 May</u>

I unpacked all the Parallel Wire apparatus and fitted it up in a shed on the other side of the house. It worked satisfactoriy and my nephew, H.J. Kemp, helped me.

<u>Monday 10 May</u>

I worked Mr Marconi's apparatus and the Parallel Wire System from 7.00 a.m. to 7.00 p.m.; the faulty drum insulation; the faulty stay insulation and the Parallel Wire system taking most of the energy to earth.

Tuesday 11 May

At 6 a.m. I refitted the mast and carried the transmitting apparatus to another direction using the drum packing case for a table. I made an aerial with four parts of G.P. covered wire 400 feet long. The mast was fitted with another set of stays 20 feet above the others. I fitted the Parallel Wire system along the top of the island instead of along the beach portion. The wires were supported on tripods to keep them clear of the ground. I then sent a few signals across to Lavernock on Mr Marconi's system but none on the Parallel Wire system. When transmitting on the four parts G.P. aerial I found the upper and lower stays sparking at the bottom due to the difference of potential between the upper and lower stays. I found the plug plate of the Parallel Wire system did not spark so much in the new position which was well clear of the masts.

Wednesday 12 May

I sent Mr Marconi's small transmitter to Professor Slaby at Lavernock, so that he could see the receiving experiments. He came on behalf of the Kaiser who had been invited by the British Post Office, and he was the only professor present at the great experiment. The signals, transmitted across to Lavernock by Mr Marconi's transmitter and the Parallel Wire system, were good. As I did not like the insulation of the drum, I sent some of the signals on the aerial which was connected to insulated stays and saw that the drum was properly insulated at night.

Thursday 13 May

The great day for the Flat Holm signals. I started at 7.00 a.m. and fitted a new copper earth wire in lieu of the iron earth. I send and received good signals on both systems between 12.00 and 1.45 p.m. The first half-hour of

V's were on a paper strip on the inker; the second, "so be it, let it be so" and the third, "it is cold here and the wind is up". This message was posted to the Kaiser by Professor Slaby.

In the afternoon Mr Marconi came over and tried some adjustments; Mr Taylor came with him and did a little transmitting but, as I sent the best sentences between 12.00 and 2.00 p.m., I returned to those adjustments and sent them the following:

"How are you"	"Send us news"
"It is hot"	"What is the time?"
"Marconi"	"Are you cold?"
"Go to bed"	"Do you read?"
"Go to Hull"	"Are you ready?"
"Go to tea"	"Do the dashes split?"
"So be it"	"Over the water"
"The tea here is good"	"Go to dinner"
"The ship has left"	(Each repeated)

Friday 14 May
Repeated some of yesterday's adjustments and tried a motor commutator with 5 amperes; the vrill break was also tried and we finished at 4.50 p.m.

Saturday 15 May
I returned to Cardiff via Penarth.

Sunday 16 May
Went to Penarth Hotel at 8 a.m. and then on to Lavernock by cab with the transmitter.

Monday 17 May
I left Cardiff for Lavernock at 8 00 a.m. and raised the kite for transmission to Brean Down. The transmission hut was about 50 yards from the house; 300 feet of wire was laid from the top of the table through an insulated shackle,

at the top of a 50 foot pole, and then on to a kite string by a piece of light aluminium with a hole in it. I then took the kite line to the top of a 107 foot pole which gave a distance of 200 feet from the ground to the aluminium plate and transmitting wire. I used six 2 volt accumulators and sent 7 amperes but, as those in charge of the station had difficulty in landing at Brean Down, and could not work the kite, we sent a Marconi message through from Brean Down to Flat Holm by cable and then by the Parallel Wire system from Flat Holm to Lavernock.

Tuesday 18 May

I repeated the above on Lavernock Point and estimated the height of the kite as follows:

Engineers reported ready on Brean Down at 2.30 p.m. and we sent at:

2.50 Vs to the right and left	2.55 "How are you"
3.00 "The kite is up and left"	3.05 "Send us news"
3.30 Vs and left	3 45-4.00 Vs
4.10-4 20 "Sky"	

They reported that they had received the messages on Brean Down.

Wednesday 19 May

I fitted up the apparatus for experiment in the field at Lavernock and received news from the engineers that they had taken my signals all correct but had no ink in the inker, consequently they kept us transmitting while they made it.

From Thursday 20 May to Wednesday 26 May

We carried out experiments in the field, with the transmitter and receiver with various lengths of wire.

From Thursday 27 May to Saturday 29 May

We transmitted between Penarth and Lavenock,

leaving Cardiff by the 10.30 p.m. train and arriving at Paddington at 3.30 a.m. on Sunday. Here we placed all the apparatus in the cloakroom.

<u>Monday 31 May</u>
Transported everything by van from the works at Holloway to the G.P.O.

The kite length was 6ft. 5ins. and the width 4ft. 2 ins bamboo vertical 1¼ in. When the bridle A is held in the hand the kite should lie in a horizontal position with a slight dip at the tail. Tail — 208 flies of brown paper 2 ft. apart with an 18 in. tassel of brown paper.

Professor Slaby represented the Kaiser at the Bristol Channel tests, and afterwards stated: "It will be for me an ineffaceable recollection. Five of us stood around the apparatus in a wooden shed . . . with eyes and ears directed towards instruments with an attention which was almost painful . . . Instantaneously we heard the first tic tac and saw. . . signals which came to us silently and invisibly from the island rock. I have seen something new. He (Marconi) was working with means the entire meaning of which no one before him had realised."

However, it does not appear that Lord Kelvin was so certain when he stated: "Telegraphy without wires is all very well, but I'd rather send a message by a boy on a pony!"

Though, perhaps, not across water.

THE CHOLERA HOSPITAL

I well remember the Cholera Hospital in the late 1950s. Even at that time there were no windows, although the roof was sound and the wood floor was complete. The small room to the right of the main entrance which originally held a portable bath had been converted by the army in 1942 to a cinema projection room and a painted screen was still on the far wall. The square holes can still be seen in the wall. The nurses' day room was in a reasonably good state of repair, with dresser and a rusting range. However the roof has been allowed to disintegrate and this has caused considerable deterioration inside the building.

An interesting history of the hospital from 1884 to 1937 has been prepared by Dr John Guy, and with his kind permission a complete account follows.

FLAT HOLM ISOLATION HOSPITAL 1884-1937

by Dr John Guy

The rapid growth of trade and commerce with all parts of the world during the 19th century, and the reduction of the length of journeys through the advent of the steamship, had together contributed towards making Asiatic cholera a world-wide problem, and the experience of the four great "cholera years" of 1831-32, 1848-49, 1853-54, and 1866 was that, although it was by no means confined to them, seaports were particularly vulnerable. In the summer of 1883 Egypt, which had come under British control following the bombardment of Alexandria in the previous year, was swept by a severe cholera epidemic.

On 12 July 1883, the Local Government Board in England issued its circular, "15,710 Cholera Regulations (General)", warning that as cholera was "now present in certain parts of Egypt with which this country has

84

communication", any ships approaching British ports with either suspected or confirmed cases of cholera on board were to be moored by direction of H.M.Customs. No one was to leave, they were to be inspected by the Port Medical Officer of Health, and sufferers were to be removed if possible "to some hospital or place previously appointed for that purpose" by the Sanitary Authority.

Three days before the issue of the Local Government Board circular, the Cardiff Borough Council had decided that "in the event of any case of cholera being imported, the same shall be treated at the Flat Holm or Sully Island". The port of Cardiff had not escaped the visitation of cholera in the earlier epidemics. There had been an aggregate of 697 deaths from the disease in 1849, 1854 and 1866. Because of this bitter experience, and its flourishing world-wide trade, Cardiff was not slow in taking precautions. By the year 1873 the port had been handling an average of 900 vessels a week, many cargoes were carried by foreign bottoms, and since the opening of the Suez Canal, Welsh coal had been shipped to India, and coaling stations en route.

The Port Sanitary Authority was acutely aware that shipping entered Cardiff from areas of the world where cholera was endemic and occasionally epidemic. Although in 1883 there was still no real understanding of its mode of transmission, the medical inspection and isolation advocated by the Local Government Board circular had by that year become increasingly favoured in Great Britain as the best way of preventing the spread of the disease, if and when it arrived.

The 1883 decision by the Borough Council established the raison d'etre of the Flat Holm Isolation Hospital for the whole of its subsequent history. It was never intended for the citizens of Cardiff, for whom an isolation hospital and sanatorium was subsequently built. The primary role was in relation to preventative medicine; it was one of the ways by which the Port Sanitary Authority hoped to stop the disease gaining a foothold in the town again.

In the event, it was another year before the island was needed. The 1883 outbreak did not spread beyond Egypt. However, in the early summer of the following year, an outbreak was reported at Toulon, which caused The Lancet to warn "that for the next few months some recrudescence of last year's cholera epidemic in Egypt is by no means an impossible occurrence". Toulon, "the French Portsmouth", enjoyed sanitary conditions which an anonymous correspondent of The Lancet described as "barbaric" and "a menace to the health of Europe". By the beginning of July, the disease had spread to Marseilles, and the Order of the Local Government Board of 12 July was re-enforced. Immediately Cardiff resumed its preparations.

Negotiations were begun with the owners of several offshore islands, Barry, Flat Holm and Steep Holm, with a view to erecting a temporary cholera hospital on one of them. The use of Barry and of Steep Holm was refused, but on 9 July J. Stuart Corbett, on behalf of the Marquess of Bute, had acceded to the Council's request. This decision immediately alarmed the firm of Elliot and Jeffery, owners of steam tugs, who handled the trade of Cardiff with the island farm. "There are all the Lambs, Fowls, Eggs, Butter, Milk and Vegetables to come to Cardiff for sale; how do you think anyone would buy them knowing they had come from alongside the Cholera Hospital?" They offered to accept £800 compensation for loss.

Undeterred, the port authority continued its preparations. From at least 10 July, the steamers approaching the port were stopped, boarded, and the authorised questions asked. The mooring ground was 1¼ to 1½ miles off Flat Holm Island. On 10 July also a telegram was despatched, requiring to know what vessels had arrived from either Toulon or Marseilles during the week. On 21 July, the Customs Officers of the port were authorised to hire the paddle-tug *Sarah and Jane*, and to employ her from the following day, to assist in the work of inspecting vessels bound for Cardiff. The hospital on the island had by then been established in readiness. On 14 July the Town Council had passed a minute to the effect that "a cholera hospital to be opened on the Flat Holm; the tenant of the farm there to be compensated for loss".

In July of 1883 the firm of Morgan & Coles of 50 Bute Street, Cardiff, had been approached in regard to the acquisition of the tents which were to provide the hospital accommodation, and probably it was these which now constituted the first hospital on the island. All that could be done had been done. The Port Authorities waited and watched.

On 30 July a telegram was received from the British Consul in Marseilles, reporting that the steamship *Rishanglys*, on passage to Cardiff, had left three behind suffering from cholera, and one had, it was believed, subsequently died. The *Rishanglys* duly arrived, with cholera on board, and the hospital came into use. By 8 September, three patients had been isolated on Flat Holm, one of whom died on the island. The use of Flat Holm was still causing concern. On 9 August the Town Clerk received a telegram from Lt.Col. Barret of the Royal Artillery at Horfield Barracks, protesting against the landing of cholera cases (from the *Rishanglys*), as there were troops stationed there, and Trinity House were also worried for their two keepers, and the risks to navigation if they succumbed to the disease and the light was extinguished as a result.

During August there were two further developments. The Port Authority at Newport requested permission to share the facilities of the island hospital, expressing a willingness to pay a proportion of the expenses, and the Council acceded to this request. The hospital was also inspected by Dr F.H. Blaxall of the Local Government

Board. Francis Henry Blaxall (MD St Andrew's; MRCS & LSA) was a retired Royal Naval Fleet Surgeon, who in 1867 had prepared a report on "The Epidemic of Malarious Fever in the Mauritius".

There is virtually no surviving information on the management of this first isolation hospital. However, the Cardiff City archives for 1884 contain among the Flat Holm papers advertisements for Phenicon, a carbolic acid disinfectant, available in various qualities (£7 per ton No 4 quality up to £10 per ton No 1 quality) and quantities. There were also one penny and two penny packets. This, presumably, was the disinfectant employed on the island.

The tented hospital continued in use into 1885, for in that year there was an outbreak of cholera in Spain at Carthagena, and a death was reported from a Cardiff steamer outward bound from that port. Once again, the city archives contain records of the precautions taken. Several vessels were offered by Cardiff companies for employment in the inspection of incoming steamers, including the *Sarah and Jane*, which had been used in 1884. In the event, on 11 July 1885 the steamtug *Earl of Windsor* was hired by the Customs. A formal agreement was drawn up with the Newport authority, and this gives some idea of the management proposed. If necessary, an Assistant Medical Officer of Health was to be appointed, to visit the ships and take charge of the hospital. The cost of his conveyance to ships in the roads and to the island, the expenses of the hospital including any necessary extensions to the premises, and the maintenance of the patients, was to be shared between Cardiff and Newport.

At the hospital care was to be taken "to provide against exposure to cold on the one hand and dampness on the other". The tents or huts were to include a separate one for a kitchen, one for the nurses, and one for the Medical Officer in charge when he had to stay. The Assistant M O H was to be in full administrative and medical charge.

Clearly the hospital was becoming at least semi-permanent, and when Dr Blaxall again inspected it, with the Mayor and Town Clerk, he expressed "great satisfaction and stated that it could not be in a better position".

The hospital does not seem to have been required after all during 1885, but the fears expressed in the previous year by Elliot and Jeffery do seem to have been justified. On 11 May the Council minutes recorded that since the cholera hospital had been established, the tenants of the island farm had suffered heavy pecuniary loss. There had been a great falling off in the moneys received from visitors (the island possessed its own inn at this time), and the farmer had experienced difficulty in selling his produce in Cardiff. Clearly, if the hospital was to continue, something of a more permanent arrangement would have to be made.

The Council entered into negotiations with the island's owner, the Marquess of Bute, and on 26 January 1886 agreed to lease it from him for £50 per annum. During that year, a permanent hospital building was provided, which was described some years later as "a shed capable of holding six beds". This early building still survives as part of the complex, as it was subsequently incorporated into the enlarged hospital to serve as an additional, auxiliary isolation ward.

The records are then silent for a number of years. The hospital was not continuously manned, but looked after by a caretaker, and it could be brought to a state of readiness as and when required. In the early 1890s the caretakers were the innkeeper and his wife. Cholera in the meantime continued to take its toll.

In 1892 there was a serious outbreak in the port of Hamburg with which Cardiff had strong trading links. The epidemic began on 16 August, and in the ensuing two months there were 18,000 recorded cases, with 8,200 deaths.

In that year, according to Cardiff's Medical Officer of Health, five infected vessels had been taken to the mooring ground off Flat Holm, and patients were removed to the hospital. The following year cholera broke out again, with recorded cases at ports such as Hull, Grimsby, Newcastle and Gloucester. This time two infected vessels were intercepted en route to Cardiff, and two cases of cholera from the SS *Blue Jacket* were removed to the hospital of the island. Sometimes, when the disease was only suspected, the patient was treated on board ship, whilst the vessel was held at the Flat Holm mooring ground. This happened in September 1892 to a crew member of the rather appropriately named French SS *Foulah.*

The Cardiff Medical Officer of Health who had been in charge of the hospital during this period came to the conclusion that the small building on the island was insufficient. This was Edward Walford (MD Durham, MRCS, LSA) who had been appointed in 1888 after a period as M O H at Ramsgate.

Walford had studied at Lyons, and was one of the earliest diplomats in Public Health. He was to devote thirty years to the city of Cardiff, publishing a number of papers based on his experience, including in 1891 *The effect of improved sanitation on the public health of seaport towns*, an address given by him to the 7th International Congress of Hygiene and Demography. In 1892 it had been necessary to erect a large marquee on the island adjacent to the hospital to afford greater space. Dr Walford wished to provide a larger permanent building. The first step towards this was a public enquiry held in Cardiff in September 1895 by an inspector of the Local Government Board, in reference to the the town council's application to borrow £2,450, the estimated cost of erecting a new hospital. Plans for the new hospital had been drawn up by the Borough Engineer and Surveyor, W. Harpur, and were outlined by him in a letter to the Town Clerk dated 13 August 1895.

The hospital, said Harpur, was intended "for the reception of cholera patients only and any person of superior social position could be isolated from the other patients by being placed in the existing small ward". He discussed the provision of down spouts; to be "directly connected to the rain water drains"; of sinks "proper slop sinks of the hospital pattern"; of fan-lights and window casements — "solid frames are more sanitary and less liable to harbour dust and disease germs". Extract ventilators should have shafts carried vertically through the roof. All of these things were, in fact, modifications of his original plans, and made in the light of comments in a letter from the Local Government Board of 3 August.

Other parts of Harpur's letter are also of interest. "The hospital being for the reception of cholera patients," he writes, "it is not at all improbable that it will be brought into use in the winter time and cold weather, but Shorelands Hospital Stoves large enough to efficiently warm the ward will be provided. There is however a difficulty in reference to the supply of hot water, as there is no fresh water procurable upon the island except what rain water may be caught and stored". This, incidentally, was an objection raised in 1884 by Elliot and Jeffery, who had pointed out that the water in the well was "only fit for cattle" and that the rainwater at the farm was sufficient only for the farm.

"All water for dietic purposes," said Harpur, "will have to be conveyed by boat to the island in barrels, and water will have at all times to be used as sparingly as possible. If a hot water boiler were provided in the range it could only be kept supplied by means of a force pump from the soft water cistern and if neglected there would be great risk of an explosion, a risk which is too serious to run. I am in hopes that we may be able to obtain instantaneous oil heaters for heating the water for baths, etc., somewhat after the character of Fletchers' Instantaneous Gas Heaters." Regarding baths, Harpur said that "the bath will be portable and the Bath Room is only intended for placing the bath in when not in use".

These facilities were to be provided in what The Lancet described as a "pavilion" comprising two six-bed wards, a nurses' room and requisite sanitary arrangements. The hospital was also to have its own crematorium.

The new hospital was also to provide facilities for the port of Barry. As the years passed, arrangements were also entered into with Barnstaple, Bridgwater and Watchet, though the contributions made towards the hospital by Barnstaple and Watchet were nominal, amounting to £1 each per annum in 1931-32.

Not only was the hospital's catchment area widened, so also was its function. In response to the Local Government Board's new regulation of 9 November 1896, the hospital was thereafter to receive not only victims of cholera, but of yellow fever and plague as well. According to Francis Knight, in October 1900 "the remains of a sailor supposed to have died from bubonic plague" were in fact cremated in the hospital's crematorium.

The remainder of the hospital's life was to be uneventful, until in July 1935 the Ministry of Health announced that it would no longer contribute to its upkeep, and condemned the building. Its accommodation — given as for 16 patients — was "no longer required". Correspondence had been going on between the City of Cardiff and the Ministry for some time and on 17 July 1935 the Health Committee decided that it was "useless in future to rely upon the hospital . . . for the isolation of cases of plague, etc., since owing to for example currents and the great rise and fall of the tides, conditions were such that frequently it would be impossible to land patients on the island". This was, of course merely a convenient excuse, as conditions were no worse in 1935 than in 1884 in these respects. The real reason was that it was felt that the Caerau Isolation Hospital, completed in 1928, could provide the necessary service.

The winding up of the hospital then began. Early in 1936 Barnstaple and Bridgwater terminated their agreements. In July the City Engineer reported that it would cost £135 to put the buildings into repair, but on 25 July the Health Committee recommended that the Council surrender its lease of the island to Messrs Mountjoy Ltd. On 3 July 1937 the appointment of Mr F.J. Harris as caretaker expired and the surrender of the island to Mountjoy Ltd. was completed three days later. The medical history of Flat Holm Island Isolation Hospital had come to an end.

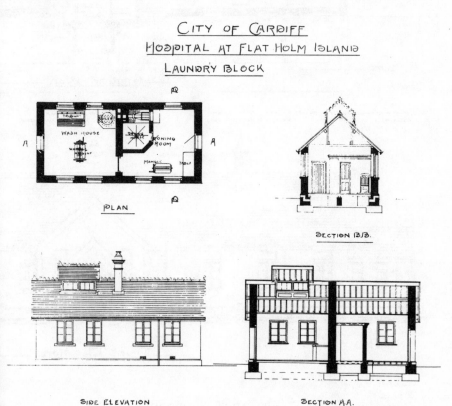

CITY OF CARDIFF

HOSPITAL AT FLAT HOLM ISLAND

LAUNDRY BLOCK

PLAN

SECTION B.B.

SIDE ELEVATION

SECTION A.A.

SCALE 8 FEET TO ONE INCH

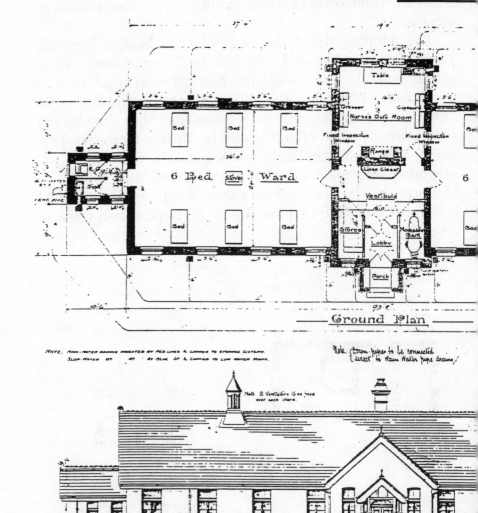

Ground Plan

NOTE. RAIN-WATER DRAINS INDICATED BY RED LINES & CARRIED TO STORAGE CISTERN.
SLOP-WATER AT AT BY BLUE AT & CARRIED TO LOW WATER MAINS.

Note. Storm-pipes to be connected
direct to Main Water pipe drains.

Front Elevation.

Note. 2 Ventilators 15 ea fixed
over each Ward.

J.W.Smith

Scale 5 feet to one Inch.

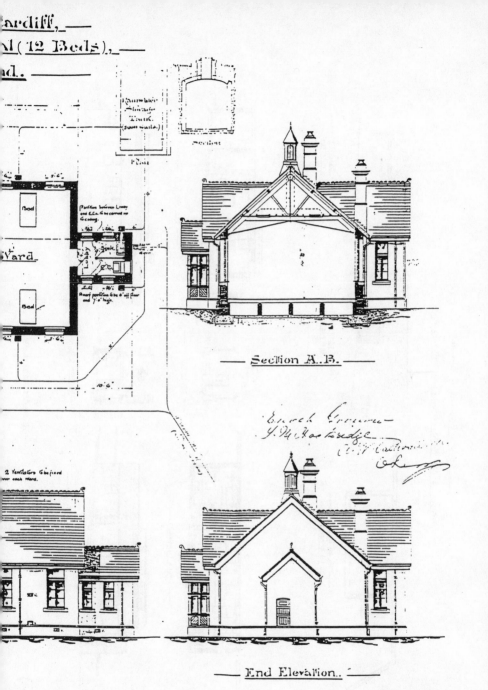

Section A.B.

End Elevation.

95

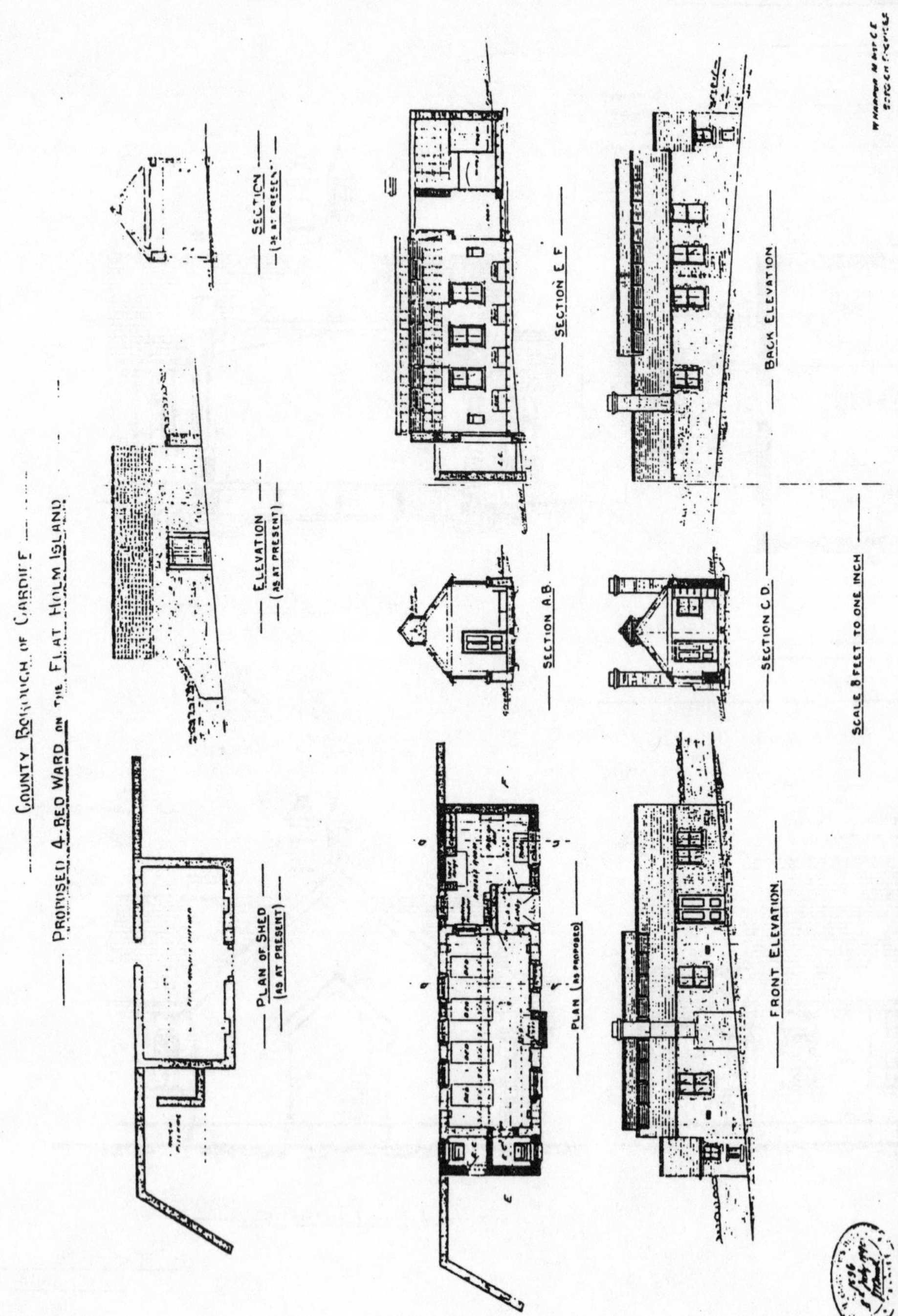

COUNTY BOROUGH OF CARDIFF

PROPOSED 4 BED WARD ON THE FLAT HOLM ISLAND

PLAN OF SHED
(AS AT PRESENT)

ELEVATION
(AS AT PRESENT)

SECTION
(AS AT PRESENT)

PLAN (AS PROPOSED)

SECTION A.B.

SECTION E.F.

SECTION C.D.

FRONT ELEVATION.

BACK ELEVATION.

SCALE 8 FEET TO ONE INCH

96

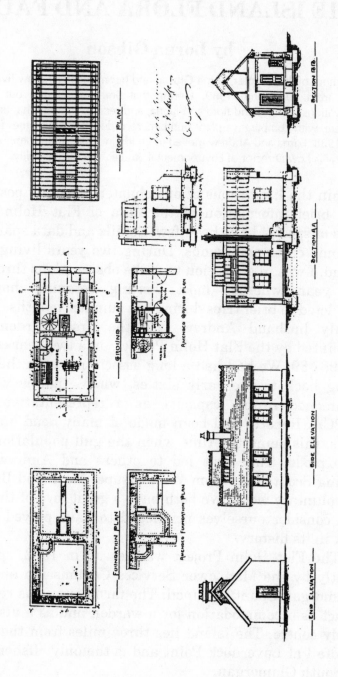

COUNTY BOROUGH OF CARDIFF

PROPOSED CHOLERA HOSPITAL AT FLAT HOLM ISLAND

ROOF PLAN

LAUNDRY BLOCK

GROUND PLAN

ANNEXED GROUND PLAN

ANNEXED SECTION AA

SECTION AA

SECTION BB

FOUNDATION PLAN

ANNEXED FOUNDATION PLAN

SIDE ELEVATION

END ELEVATION

THE ISLAND FLORA AND FAUNA

by Lorna Gibson

The author of this chapter, Lorna Gibson and her husband Andrew lived on Flat Holm from 1987 until 1989. During that time she carried out extensive observations of the island flora and fauna, and records up until that time are set out here, with comparative plant numbers recorded at various times from 1890 until 1988. Lorna and Andrew moved to Lundy in 1989, their home until 1994. Andrew is now Director of Environmental Studies, the Isles of Scilly.

Within the limitations of one chapter it is only possible to give brief information of the flora of Flat Holm Island. Lists of species have been few, details and data sparse, and in some cases ambiguous. During two years living on the island, I was in a position to make observations throughout the year, whereas most visiting botanists had been restricted to brief trips during the summer months.

My husband Andrew was the first Warden to be appointed by the Flat Holm Project, on a two year contract, in 1987-89. We had had a long association with the island, going back to the early sixties, when Andrew was first summoned in his capacity as a representative of the RSPCA. Reports had been made of many dead and dying gulls, this being the time when the gull population began to explode. This visit led to others and Andrew began taking Scouts over from Weston-super-Mare and Bristol to do voluntary work. We both have a great love of the island and consider ourselves privileged to have played a small part in its history.

The Flat Holm Project was set up in 1982, sponsored jointly by the Manpower Services Commission and South Glamorgan County Council. The farmhouse was renovated to act as accommodation for a warden and as a visitor and study centre. The island lies three miles from the nearest landfall at Lavernock Point and is the only offshore island in South Glamorgan.

This last inhabited limestone outcrop of the Mendip Hills has seen many changes in use including mining, farming, and fortification, which have all had their effect on the vegetation. The greatest opportunity for introductions probably occurred during the Second World War occupation when some 350 army personnel were stationed on Flat Holm. Seeds could have been carried on equipment, sandbags and so on. Other species would have suffered from the building work and the trampling of so many pairs of feet.

Before the war, farming and market gardening had been carried out by the Harris family. Following the army occupation, when Commander Knowles took on the lease, visitors were encouraged, as they had been in the pre-war heyday of the paddle-steamers, and once more trippers landed in large numbers. This, together with rabbit grazing, helped to keep the maritime sward in good condition. As this activity declined, and land management ceased, the gradual encroachment of scrub began and gull numbers soared, reaching a peak of 8,000 breeding pairs by the mid-seventies. By the time we lived there, large areas of the plateau were dominated by ragwort, bracken and thistles. Elder and brambles had spread too. These, though in need of control, had the advantage of providing cover for birds. The gull population had declined to around 2,000 pairs, but the colony was widespread. The guano left the soil acid, especially in dry seasons, and vegetation was burnt and trampled, leaving large bare areas. Litter left behind after the breeding season proved that a major source of scavenged food was mainland rubbish tips, with chicken bones and giblet bags strewn everywhere. This was a dramatic change from the golf-course-like appearance reported in earlier years.

Control was needed and an extensive regime of cutting and spraying the ragwort had been embarked upon by the Flat Holm Project. However, in small areas where pulling was tried the result was an immediate regeneration of grass. During the sixties, six goats grazed the island and helped keep some of the vegetation in check, but they were harassed by gulls and eventually succumbed to the hazards of the cliff edges. Recently goats have been re-introduced and are kept on the area which is being managed.

A problem encountered, whilst leading guided tours, was that stragglers needed to be carefully watched, as it was quite tempting for people to pick off seed heads, particularly of the attractive Wild Leek, and quietly slip them into their pockets. The seeds, likely to be unripe, would not have germinated, thus rendering it a futile act of vandalism.

Although the Flat Holm flora is unremarkable, with the exception of the rare Wild Leek and also rare, though introduced, Wild Peony, the succession of colour through the seasons is quite a spectacle. Bluebells, Sea Campion, Thrift, Wallflowers, Bird's-foot Trefoil, Wild Turnip and even the demon Ragwort create carpets of colour in their turn and attract bees and butterflies. The south-west of the island is topped by a springy turf and hummocks of salt-tolerant Thrift, whilst rock crevices are preferred by Sea Lavender and Scurvygrass.

The rainfall is significantly less than that of the nearby coastline, but the island is subject to sea mist and high insolation (exposure to the sun's rays). The prevailing south-westerly winds, which often reach gale force, cause dwarfing of some species while others only survive in the lee of the higher ground to the east. The lower ground to the south and west is subject to sea spray and here salt tolerant plants grow which are not otherwise found so far up the Bristol Channel.

An interesting phenomenon is the number of plants which are normally pink or blue, but on Flat Holm also appear in white form. This appears to be a common occurrence on islands, with no known explanation.

Knight's theory (*Heart of Mendip,* 1915, p.143) that lead-ore contaminated soil is responsible for flowers turning white is questionable, since this also occurs where lead is not present, though lead mining did take place on Flat Holm.

Flat Holm was designated a Site of Special Scientific Interest in 1972 and it became a Local Nature Reserve in 1975 when South Glamorgan County Council took on a 99 year lease.

Cultivation

The fertile soil has been cultivated many times, and it is interesting to speculate whether some of the plants on the island today could have been introduced for culinary, medicinal or other purposes. The Wild Leek is an obvious contender for the culinary possibility, as are the more humble Dandelion, Sorrel, Hawthorn, Elder and Sloe. Plants with medicinal properties include Nettle, Chickweed, Yarrow, Common St John's Wort and Cleavers. Henbane, a poisonous plant, the roots of which were once used as a teething necklace, is described (*Plants with a Purpose* Richard Mabey, 1977) as being "similar in effect to hemlock, but is a stronger narcotic and can give rise to insensibility more quickly". Salad Burnet, Violet, Mint, Cowslip and Daisy were all useful as strewing herbs and the leaves of Great Mullein could be used as tinder, wicks or tobacco. Burdock leaves would have made butter wrappers, Bracken bedding or dye, and Bluebells glue or starch for laundering. There are many other beneficial plants of the island with a variety of uses. According to old maps, there was a friars' garden, and this would probably have been established at the time St Cadoc used Flat Holm as a retreat in the sixth century.

Gardeners through the ages would have had to contend with salt-laden winds and a limited water supply. One advantage, to counteract the exposed conditions, is that very few frosts occur. Crops would have been vital to the survival of many an islander, since it is possible to be cut off for weeks at a time. Rabbits, besides providing food, must have proved a headache to many an exasperated gardener, but slow-worms on the other hand would have been an asset, by eating slugs and other garden pests.

The early Lighthouse keepers and their families lived in now demolished cottages, attached to the base of the tower. Nearby were pig sties and gardens, some walls of which remain intact, though the gardens have long since been abandoned. When the island was declared a rock station and families no longer allowed to live there, keepers moved to their new quarters beside the foghorn station. They grew their vegetables, within the boundary walls, as meticulously as they carried out their duties, and their lawns were always orderly and well manicured.

During the construction and occupation of the Victorian Barracks, gardens were created between the defensive ditch and where the foghorn station now stands. The water catchment area, constructed to serve the barracks, covers a former potato patch.

During the Second World War, with the exception of the farmhouse garden in which a half-size Nissen hut was built, much use was made of the gardens. No doubt these provided a welcome diversion and fresh produce for the occupying forces. There is still evidence of borders on the sheltered side of some wartime buildings.

The Harris family were tenants of the farm from the 1890s until the second world war and for part of this time the farmhouse became the Flatholm Hotel. Members of the family recall the garden behind it was laid to lawn with Star of Bethlehem growing beneath an apple tree. On the raised garden which extends along the west wall grew rose bushes, a few of which still survive, along with Lilac, Fuchsia and Duke of Argyll's Teaplant. Dr A.T.J. Dollar, on an archaeological visit in April 1936, noticed the leaves of Bluebells in evidence everywhere. He also noted: "The 'roads' between the Batteries are distinguished by fine, brilliant and relatively weed-free turf."

At the farm he was introduced to Mr Frank Harris, who told him a Myrtle used to live in his garden, but did so no longer. He thought people took so many pieces away that it died. In 1890, T.H. Thomas and John Storrie noted a Barberry beside Harris's house, and two Sycamores in the shelter of the garden wall, all planted. A stunted apple grew in the ditch at the lighthouse and *Iris germanica* — pale purple variety, one group, probably an escape from the lighthouse garden. Is it possible that this was in fact *I. foetidissima*, Stinking Iris, which has appeared on every subsequent list?

After the war, prisoners of war remained to demolish verious redundant constructions They were there until 1946. The lease was taken on by Ronald Knowles until it ran out in 1975, though he stopped visiting the island in the early sixties. From the end of the war until we moved into the renovated farmhouse in 1987, no cultivation of that area seems to have taken place. With the help of many volunteers, we cleared thick brambles, rubble, large pieces of rusty corrugated iron and assorted debris. After much backbreaking work I was proud of my efforts as a novice gardener, when I produced crops of potatoes, carrots, onions, leeks and tomatoes. With no end wall at that time, my lettuce and flower border succumbed to the ravages of south-westerlies, and the rabbits soon discovered where they could find tasty variety in their diet. To me, the weeds which appeared in the disturbed soil were of as much interest as the vegetables, and many were allowed to survive. Previously unrecorded species were Many-seeded Goosefoot and Black Bindweed Three varieties of Fumitory grew in close proximity.

Now things have moved on apace and the Victorian garden which had been envisaged is a reality. We are pleased to hear that some of our ideas have been incorporated into this scheme. The raised garden is now a walkway with a herb garden, and from a platform at the far end, the site of an old earth closet, panoramic views are to be had. A pergola separates the cultivated section from the wild area. Various plants including the Wild Peony and the Wild Leek are there to be studied.

FLAT HOLM FAUNA

Rabbits have long been established on the island, introduced for profit as far back as the twelfth or thirteenth century. The earliest record of a warren was in 1236, on Lundy Island, some 65 miles down the Bristol Channel, and it is likely they were taken to Flat Holm at about the same time. Myxomatosis regularly reduces rabbit numbers and can deplete the population by up to two-thirds. However they seem to have a remarkable capacity to "bounce back", and average population is around seven hundred.

The Black (or Ship) Rat has been a problem in the past. Lighthouse keepers, who were adept at telling colourful stories, recalled seeing "hundreds of pairs of eyes" watching them as they walked at night, between their quarters and the Lighthouse. "There was some truth in these stories," says Robert Jory. "When I stayed on the island some 35 years ago rat-catching was something of a sport. A dozen large traps similar to the small mouse traps placed around the farmhouse would be set off in a matter of minutes."

However a pest control officer was called in and did a very effective job. The only rats we found were two mummified ones in Lighthouse Battery.

Pipistrelle bats are often seen on warm summer evenings, though never more than two or three at a time. They are thought to roost in underground shelters or disused buildings.

There are good numbers of slow-worms and these are distinguished from the mainland variety by a more pronounced blue fleck on adult specimens. They bask in the warmth provided under slates and corrugated iron. The common lizard inhabits the warmer south-eastern side of the island between Coal Beach and the lighthouse.

Although birdlife is dominated by the gull colony the plateau is also a nesting place for a variety of birds including thrush, blackbird, robin, wren and meadow pipit. Rock pipits nest in the inaccessible crevices in the rocks and up to seven pairs of oystercatchers nest around the coastline. Lesser black-backed gulls prefer the plateau and herring gulls favour rocks above the tide-line, though there is a certain amount of overlapping. Two or three pairs of great black-backed gulls breed on the eastern cliffs. Shelduck numbers are on the increase, nesting in rabbit burrows, giving rise to their other name, burrow-ducks.They are most attractive and interesting birds whose head bobbing rituals can be observed in the early morning on top of the Batteries and Command posts, where they hold their "parliaments".

During migration, birds use the island as a resting place and sometimes rarities are seen, especially after storms. In autumn, thousands of starlings feed on the elderberries, turning the top of the Lighthouse tower purple with their droppings. Large flocks of goldfinch and other seed-eaters are attracted by ragwort and thistles. The island is also used as a roost for waders such as dunlin, purple sandpiper, turnstone and oystercatcher. At dusk it is a breathtaking sight to see large flocks of dunlin wheeling and diving low over the sea, prior to settling for the night. Noisy oystercatchers too flock together and sometimes on calm nights in early spring perform shrill piping rituals in front of the farmhouse. When storm-bound, waders huddle together on the rocks, finding what shelter they can from the crashing waves. Cormorants often pass but seldom land, ravens frequently visit from the Welsh coast and kestrels are a common sight. The occasional grey heron is mobbed by furious gulls as it looks for easy pickings.

THE LISTS

Early records of the flora of Flat Holm are few, though the island was inhabited and boats would have crossed the Bristol Channel frequently. Botanists seemed to have been more attracted to Steep Holm, the site of the rare *Paeonia mascula*, Wild Peony.

The earliest list I have included was compiled by T.H. Thomas and John Storrie in June 1890, during expeditions organised by Cardiff Naturalists' Society. An account of these visits was given to the society by F.W. Wooton in November of the year and was published in their *Report and Transactions* Vol. XXII Part II 1890. The parties departed from Penarth in the chartered 1,000 pound craft *Renown*, commanded by Captain Harris. Three visits in all were made and passengers in addition to Messrs. Thomas and Storrie included Messrs. Neale, West, T.W. Proger and F.W. Wootton.

In his report, F.W. Wootton quotes John Rutter, from 1829: "This Island, which is about the same size as Steep Holme, is about three miles north of it. There is an inn and a homestead to a dairy farm of 60 acres, the land bearing good crops and abounding with burnet, wild thyme and other aromatic plants. The inn is occasionally honoured by a visit from the corporation of Bristol, whose judicial rights extend as far as this down the channel. There is good bathing upon the pebbly beach, which at low water extends all round the island . . . great numbers of sea anemones of different kinds are left on the beach when the tide is out, and on the south side are large turbulated ones which, when open, are six inches in diameter. There is a remarkable well of fresh water here, which when the sea ebbs is filled, but when it flows is empty."

Wootton comments: "Rutter evidently did not write from personal observation, as the description given by him is identical with that given in Collinson's *History and Antiquities of the County of Somerset* [1791], and Collinson is the older writer, Rutter must have copied, and Collinson may have done the same thing, his observations not being altogether correct, or else the island must have undergone many changes. The only bit of pebbly beach to be seen now is on the north side, which is the sole landing place and about the only spot where bathing could be indulged in with safety, combined with comfort, unless the boots were kept on, or the bather was pachydermatous."

A visit organised by Cardiff Naturalists' Society in June 1932 comprised A.J. Wilmott, Keeper of Botany at the British Museum (Nat.Hist.) and other eminent botanists Dr H.A. Hyde, Prof. R.C. Mclean, Miss E Vachell and A.E. Wade. This resulted in a list produced by Dr Hyde with acknowledgements to Miss Vachell for use of her notes, and which included 20 additions by A.J. Wilmott.

The 1963 list also includes some species recorded in 1964. In both years visits were made by the Extra Mural Department, University College of South Wales and Monmouthshire, led by Dr Mary Gillam. The records they compiled were compared with those of Thomas and Storrie (1890). It is unclear, however, which plants were seen both in 1890 and 1963/4. I have omitted several species where I have been reliably assured that they had disappeared by the sixties.

In 1967, S.G.S. Harrison and A.E. Wade, National Museum of Wales, produced *Notes on the Flora of Flat*

Holm and a list showing comparisons with 1932 and 1963/4. The total number of species recorded at this time was 222 which included some earlier records not confirmed in the later lists. This report points out that these lists cannot be expected to be comprehensive as each resulted from a one-day visit to the island.

The 1979 list is taken from *Flat Holm — A study*, which was updated in 1980. This was based on notes prepared by Dr Mary Gillam in 1974. The 1983 list is mainly of species growing within 50 metres of the coast. This gives locations and abundance which there is no space to include here. Another list in 1986 gives some data on abundance and locations. Unfortunately neither of these lists are signed and no further information seems available. They could possibly have been the work of students doing research on the island.

I have drawn on all these earlier lists when compiling my own list of Flora which covers the years 1987/88. Christopher Cornell also produced lists for these years which were very similar to my own. He has kindly agreed that I may use his 1987 list with my additions and my 1988 list with his additions. My list includes ferns but not grasses.

Caper Spurge, Water Mint, Pepermint, Zig-zag Clover and Common Saltmarsh Grass were all included on an unsigned and undated list headed *A Flat Holm Species list — compiled from past records*.

Notes on individual species (in alphabetical order).

Aesculus hippocastanum — Horse Chestnut. In the mid-seventies a Lighthouse-keeper, George Doyle, had the idea of planting trees, creating a garden with a fish pond and releasing small animals in the defensive ditch surrounding the Lighthouse. This scheme was doomed to failure because the trees he ordered were left unwatered at the Trinity

House Depot in Swansea and arrived on Flat Holm either dead or very near so. The animals also perished, with the exception of one tortoise out of seven. The tortoise having survived an attempt to smuggle him off the island was, in the late 1980s, still appearing each spring at the keepers' back door for a wash and brush-up. Evidence of the excavation for the pond can still be seen. A single horse chestnut survives, though its growth is severely stunted by salt-laden south-westerly winds.

Allium ampeloprasum — Wild Leek. This rare plant, which grows to a height of 1.8 metres, is mainly restricted to Steep Holm, Flat Holm, Cornwall, Pembrokeshire and the Mediterranean. It was first mentioned by John Ray (*Ray Synopsis methodica stirpium Britannicarum* Ed.1 p. 165, 1690), and later by Rev J. Lightfoot, growing by the landing stage — H.J. Riddlesdell (*Lightfoot's journey to Wales in 1773.* Journal of Botany, 43. p.290-307, 1905). In direct conflict, Knight (*Seaboard of Mendip,* 1902) states that neither Wild Leek nor Wild Peony occurred at this time. [They were only on Steep Holm].

As reported by J.W. White (*Flora of Bristol,* 1912):
Perfectly naturalised on the Steep Holm, where it seems to have been abundant in the seventeenth century as it is now in the twentieth. Together with the Peony this has been assumed, perhaps too rashly, to be an "introduction".
The earliest record is by Ray (*Historia Plantarum* p.1126, 1688) as "Allium montanum majus, Newtoni". A few years later,in 1696, Ray described this Leek in his *Synopsis of the Plants of Britain* as "Allium Holmense splaerico capite. Great round-headed Garlic of the Holms-Island. In parva quadam insula *Holms* dicta in Sabrinae aestuario copiose provenientem observavit Dr James Newton".

The Rev H.J. Riddlesdell (*Flora of Glamorgan,* p.87, c. 1902) mentions a specimen from Flat Holm in *Herbarium of the British Museum.* He reports it also from Porthkerry. A good patch was discovered on Minehead Warren in 1906 by the Rev E.S. Marshall, who considered it certainly not an escape from cultivation but possibly water-borne from Steep Holm.

In June 1891, I saw this fine species in plenty upon a rocky slope at the Holm, and obtained herbarium specimens from two bulbs which flowered in the garden the year following. These, unluckily, did not long survive.

"Considered by some botanists to be the ancestor of the cultivated Leek, by others to be a degenerate survivor from the monkish garden known to have existed somewhere on the island: the monks, if Welshmen, would surely raise a supply of the national emblem." — John Storrie.

Mr Borrer and Prof. Babington both concluded that the presence of the plant upon Steep Holm was due to former cultivation. It does not appear to differ specifically from *A. porrum.*

In 1988, as part of a survey of this species, I helped Vicky Morgan of the Nature Conservancy Council to plot the distribution of the plant on the island. The count revealed approximately 250 flower heads, plus 46 known, or thought to be, transplants. The greatest concentration of these was in the south-eastern quarter.

Amsinkia lycopsoides — Fiddleneck. Found in rubbish tipped from the farmhouse.

Carlina vulgaris — Carline Thistle. This thistle was common in 1890 but is now only found in small stands near the lighthouse.

Cheiranthus cheiri — Wallflower. In 1890, one plant was recorded, near the Lighthouse. Now, in spring, the whole cliff below the Lighthouse is covered in a sea of golden-yellow wallflowers. They also appear elsewhere, in old walls and rock crevices, mainly near the Lighthouse.

Chenopodium polyspermum — Many-seeded Goosefoot. Appeared in disturbed soil in the farmhouse garden.

Circium acaule — Dwarf Thistle. I came upon about five plants by chance, almost obscured by grass, beside the path to Coal Beach, in the bank of a small quarry, whilst introducing a girl from Trinidad to our small flowers. (She was more used to the large and flamboyant flowers of the tropics and was delighted by their miniature perfection).

Convolvulus arvensis — Field Bindweed. This sometimes appears in the area between the farmhouse and the steps to the jetty.

Coronopus didymus — Lesser Swinecress. Two plants near the Barracks.

Epilobium species — Willowherb. I found the basal rosette of an Epilobium sp. on the capping of a rainwater storage chamber just to the south east of the cholera hospital and managed to photograph it, but by the next day it had been eaten off.

Erodium cicutarium ssp. cicutarium— Common Stork's-bill. This is locally frequent and grows approximately 30m south of the former keepers' quarters.

Fallopia convolvulus — Black Bindweed. On the high walkway in the farmhouse garden in disturbed soil.

Fuchsia magellanica - Fuchsia. This has been included in the list, for although it was clearly planted, it has survived unattended for many years.

Gagea lutea — Yellow Star-of-Bethlehem. This was almost certainly an error and should have been *Ornithogalum umbellatum* — Star-of Bethlehem.

Impatiens glandulifera — Indian Balsam. This plant has been omitted from the lists as it was a mis-identification.

Had it been this invasive species, the policy of spraying would probably have been justified, but the plant was in fact Common Figwort, which defied all attempts to exterminate it.

Inula conzya — Ploughman's Spikenard. Only one plant in the bank of the defensive ditch.

Lycium barbarum — Duke of Argyll's Teaplant. Like the Fuchsia, I include this because it has survived in the farmhouse garden unattended.

Malva neglecta — Dwarf Mallow. Found at the foot of the steps on the World War II hospital base.

Narcissus species — Both Daffodil and Narcissus occur in the vicinity of the farmhouse, and below the Lighthouse on a steep bank to the east is a bank of daffodils. All probably garden escapes.

Ophrys apifera — *Bee Orchid*. The only record is by Banks and Lightfoot, 1773.

Ornithogalum umbellatum — Star-of-Bethlehem. This now only grows in a grassy bank and "lawn" on the seaward side of the Lighthouse, near the gun emplacement.

Paeonia mascula — Peony. Introduced to Flat Holm from Steep Holm by Frank Harris, there were were a reported 36 plants in 1941. Mr Harris, who crossed frequently between the islands, is said to have often returned with "another peony". After the World War II occupation, the numbers had dwindled. In the 1980s the one remaining plant, beside the path to the Lighthouse, was protected by wire and seeds taken to the mainland for propagation. A single plant was spotted in the Trinity House garden, but this disappeared when the light was automated and the keepers left. In 1988, following the clearance of rubble on the seaward side of the farmhouse garden wall, a magnificent double peony appeared. It was clearly of garden origin.

Papaver rhoeas — Common Poppy. This occurred in disturbed soil near the Lighthouse but has been seen elsewhere at various times.

P. somniferum — Opium Poppy. This occurred within a few feet of the Common Poppy above.

Polygala vulgaris — Common Milkwort. This is one of the species which seems to have suffered from wartime occupation. It was common in 1890 (coloured from white to deep blue but not purple), and was still present in 1932, but is no longer found.

Ranunculus parviflorus — Small-flowered Buttercup. Very few, on the banks of the defensive ditch, west of the Lighthouse.

Rhamus frangula — Alder Buckthorn. (*R. catharticus* — Purging Buckthorn, given by Dr Turton, not seen 1980). This report leads me to wonder if a plant I did not identify could be this species. It grows in a depression, probably an old mine-shaft, to the south-west of the foghorn station

Senecio bicolor — Silver Ragwort. This may have been an escape from the keepers' garden, as it occurs in crevices in rocks below the water catchment area, which is near the old gardens.

Silene vulgaris — Bladder Campion. On the earliest list, this and Sea Campion were reported to be common, though in subsequent lists only the latter is mentioned.

Sisymbrium officinale — Hedge Mustard. In the farmhouse garden and above the jetty.

Smyrnium olusatrum — Alexanders. This plant has not survived on Flat Holm unlike the neighbouring island of Steep Holm where it has long been recorded and is dominant in most parts. It was recorded by Trown in 1911.

Syringia vulgaris — Lilac. Several plants have survived in the farmhouse garden.

Tamus communis — Black Briony. One plant to the east of the keepers' quarters and another beyond the eastern end of the defensive ditch.

Trifolium ornothopioides — Bird's-foot Clover (formerly Fenugreek). Locally common on paths.

Phillitis scolopendrium — Hartstongue. Only one plant was found, but this perished in spite of attempts to re-establish it, when the cover of rainwater catchment tank at the rear of the farmhouse was removed.

ACKNOWLEDGEMENTS

My grateful thanks for their help in compiling this chapter to R.Gwynn Ellis, Department of Botany, National Museum of Wales, Stan and Joan Rendell, Weston-super-Mare, Christopher Cornell, Yeovil, Jonathan Jones, Caerphilly, Maggy Gee, London.

Wild Leeks,
drawn by Lorna Gibson.

		1890	1932	1963	1967	1979	1983	1986	1987	1988	
Acer pseudoplatanus	Sycamore	█		█	█	█		█	█	█	
Achillea millefolium	Yarrow	█	█	█	█	█		█	█	█	
Aegopodium podagraria	Ground-elder		█								
Aesculus hippocastanum	Horse-chestnut		█								
Aethusa cynapium	Fool's Parsley										
Agrimonia eupatoria	Agrimony										
Allium ampeloprasum	Wild Leek	█	█	█	█	█	█	█	█	█	
Amsinkia lycopsoides	Fiddleneck										
Anagallis arvensis	Scarlet Pimpernel	█	█	█	█	█		█	█	█	
Aphanes arvensis	Parsley Piert	█		█							
Arctium lappa	Greater Burdock	█									
A. minus	Lesser Burdock	█		█	█	█		█	█	█	
Arenaria serpyllifolia	Thyme-leaved Sandwort						█	█	█	█	
Armeria maritima ssp. maritima	Thrift	█		█	█	█	█	█	█	█	
Arum maculatum	Lords-and-Ladies										
Atriplex glabriuscula	Babington's Orache	█		█		█		█	█	█	
A. patula	Common Orache	█		█	█	█		█	█	█	
A. prostrata	Spear-leaved Orache	█		█		█		█	█	█	
Bellis perennis	Daisy	█		█	█	█		█	█	█	
Berberis vulgaris	Barberry		█								
Beta vulgaris ssp. vulgaris	Sea Beet	█	█	█	█	█		█	█	█	
Blackstonia perfoliata	Yellow-wort										
Brassica napus	Rape		█								
B. oleracea	Wild Cabbage			█	█	█		█	█	█	
B. rapa	Wild Turnip	█									
Calamintha sylvatica ssp. ascendens	Common Calamint										
Calluna vulgaris	Heather		█								
Capsella bursa-pastoris	Shepherd's-purse	█	█	█	█	█		█	█	█	
Cardamine hirsuta	Hairy Bitter-cress			█	█	█		█	█	█	
Carduus acanthoides	Welted Thistle										
C. tenuiflorus	Slender Thistle	█		█	█	█		█	█	█	
Carlina vulgaris	Carline Thistle										
Centaurea nigra ssp. nemoralis	Common Knapweed	█		█	█	█	█	█	█	█	
C. scabiosa	Greater Knapweed						█				
Centaurium erythraea	Common Centaury	█		█	█	█	█	█	█	█	
Centranthus ruber	Red Valerian					█		█	█	█	
Cerastium arvense	Field Mouse-ear	█		█	█	█	█	█	█	█	
C. diffusum	Sea Mouse-ear	█			█			█	█	█	
C. fontanum	Common Mouse-ear	█	█	█	█	█		█	█	█	
C. glomeratum	Sticky Mouse-ear			█	█	█		█	█	█	
C. semidecandrum	Little Mouse-ear	█	█	█	█	█		█	█	█	
Cheiranthus cheiri	Wallflower	█					█	█	█	█	
Chenopodium album	Fat Hen	█	█	█	█	█		█	█	█	
C. polyspermum	Many-seeded Goosefoot								█	█	

115

		1890	1932	1963	1967	1979	1983	1986	1987	1988
C. rubrum	Red Goosefoot								■	■
Cirsium acaule	Dwarf Thistle								■	■
C. arvense	Creeping Thistle		■		■	■	■	■	■	■
C. vulgare	Spear Thistle		■		■	■	■	■	■	■
Clinopodium vulgare	Wild Basil	■		■						
Cocleria anglica	English Scurvygrass								■	■
C. danica	Danish Scurvygrass							■	■	■
C. officinalis	Common Scurvygrass	■				■	■		■	■
Conium maculatum	Hemlock								■	■
Convolvulus arvensis	Field Bindweed	■							■	■
Coronopus didymus	Lesser Swinecress								■	■
Crataegus monogyna	Hawthorn		■	■					■	■
Crepis capillaris	Smooth Hawksbeard				■				■	■
C. vesicaria	Beaked Hawksbeard								■	■
Crithmum maritimum	Rock Samphire	■							■	■
Cynoglossum officinale	Hound's-tongue								■	■
Daucus carota	Wild Carrot	■							■	■
Digitalis purpurea	Foxglove		■						■	■
Dipsacus fullonum	Teasel	■							■	■
Echium vulgare	Viper's-bugloss	■							■	■
Epilobium tetragonum	Square-stalked Willowherb								■	■
Erodium cicutarium ssp. cicutarium	Common Stork's-bill								■	■
E. maritimum	Sea Stork's-bill	■							■	■
Eryngium maritimum	Sea-holly								■	■
Euphorbia lathyrus	Caper Spurge								■	■
Euphrasia nemorosa	Eyebright sp.			■					■	■
E. officinalis	Eyebright	■				■			■	■
E. tetraquetra	Broad-leaved Eyebright			■		■			■	■
Fallopia convolvulus	Black Bindweed								■	■
Foeniculum vulgare	Fennel	■							■	■
Frangula alnus	Alder Buckthorn								■	
Fuchsia magellanica	Fuchsia							■	■	■
Fumaria bastardii	Tall Ramping-fumitory			■					■	■
F. capreolata	White Ramping-fumitory	■							■	■
F. muralis	Common Ramping-fumitory	■							■	■
F. officinalis	Common Fumitory	■							■	■
Gagea lutea	Yellow Star-of-Bethlehem						■			
Galium aparine	Cleavers		■						■	■
G. mollugo	Hedge-bedstraw	■					■		■	■
G. saxatile	Heath Bedstraw		■					■	■	■
G. verum	Lady's Bedstraw	■					■	■	■	■
Gentianella amarella	Autumn Gentian								■	■
Geranium dissectum	Cut-leaved Crane's-bill		■						■	■
G. molle	Dove's-foot Crane's-bill	■		■				■	■	■

116

	1890	1932	1963	1967	1979	1983	1986	1987	1988
G. robertianum — Herb Robert	■	■	■			■	■	■	■
Glechoma hederacea — Ground-ivy	■	■	■		■		■	■	■
Hedera helix — Ivy	■	■	■		■		■	■	■
Heracleum spondylium — Hogweed	■	■	■		■	■	■	■	■
Hyacinthoides hispanica — Spanish Bluebell						■		■	■
H. non-scripta — Bluebell	■	■		■			■	■	■
Hyoscyamus niger — Henbane	■		■				■		
Hypericum perforatum — Perforate St. John's-wort	■	■		■	■		■	■	■
H. pulchrum — Slender St. John's-wort	■								
Hypochaeris radicata — Cat's-ear	■	■		■		■	■	■	■
Inula conyza — Ploughman's Spikenard	■	■					■		
Iris foetidissima — Stinking Iris	■	■		■		■	■	■	■
Iris germanica — Flag Iris							■		
Lamium purpureum — Red Dead-nettle	■	■	■		■	■	■	■	■
Lavertera arborea — Tree Mallow	■	■					■		
Leontodon autumnalis — Autumn Hawkbit	■	■					■	■	
L. hispidus — Rough Hawkbit	■	■					■		
L. taraxacoides — Lesser Hawkbit	■	■		■					
Lepidium campestre — Field Pepperwort	■	■		■					
Leucanthemum vulgare — Oxeye Daisy	■	■	■		■	■	■	■	■
Ligustrum vulgare — Wild Privet	■	■	■		■		■	■	■
Limonium binervosum — Rock Sea-lavender									
L. vulgare — Common Sea-lavender									
Linum catharticum — Fairy Flax	■	■					■		
Lotus corniculatus — Common Bird's-foot-trefoil	■	■	■		■	■	■	■	■
Luzula campestris — Field Wood-rush	■	■					■		
Lycium barbarum — Duke of Argyll's Teaplant									
Malus sylvestris — Crab Apple	■								
Malva neglecta — Dwarf Mallow	■	■		■			■		
M. sylvestris — Common Mallow	■	■	■		■	■	■	■	■
Marrubium vulgare — White Horehound	■	■					■		
Medicago lupulina — Black Medick	■	■					■	■	
Mentha aquatica — Water Mint									
M. arvensis — Corn Mint		■					■		
M. spicata — Spear Mint									
M. x piperata — Peppermint									
Mercuralis annua — Annual Mercury		■					■		
Myosotis arvensis — Field Forget-me-not		■		■			■		
M. ramosissima — Early Forget-me-not						■	■		
Narcissus sp. — Daffodil									
Narcissus sp. — Narcissus									■
Ophrys apifera — Bee Orchid									
Origanum vulgare — Marjoram	■								
Ornithogalum umbellatum — Star-of-Bethlehem			■					■	■

117

	1890	1932	1963	1967	1979	1983	1986	1987	1988
Orobanche elatior — Knapweed Broomrape					■				
O. hederae — Ivy Broomrape								■	
O. sp. — Broomrape			■						
Paeonia mascula — Peony							■		
P. sp. — Garden Peony							■		
Papaver rhoeas — Common Poppy									
P. somniferum — Opium Poppy									
Parietaria judaica — Pellitory-of-the-wall		■	■						
Pimpinella saxifraga — Burnet-saxifrage				■					
Plantago coronopus — Buck's-horn Plantain	■	■							
P. lanceolata — Ribwort Plantain	■	■	■	■					
P. major — Greater Plantain	■	■			■				
P. maritima — Sea Plantain	■			■		■			
Polygala oxyptera — Milkwort								■	
P. vulgaris — Common Milkwort	■								
Polygonum aviculare agg. — Knotgrass			■						
Potentilla reptans — Creeping cinqufoil	■	■							
Primula veris — Cowslip	■			■		■			
P. vulgaris — Primrose	■								
Prunella vulgaris — Selfheal	■	■							
Prunus spinosa — Blackthorn	■	■	■						
Pulicaria dysenterica — Common Fleabane					■				
Ranunculus bulbosus — Bulbous Buttercup		■	■						
R. ficaria — Lesser Celandine	■								
R. parviflorus — Small-flowered Buttercup							■		
R. repens — Creeping Buttercup	■	■	■						
Reseda luteola — Weld	■								
Rhamus catharticus — Buckthorn	■								
Rosa canina — Dog Rose	■	■							
R. rubiginosa — Sweet-briar	■				■				
Rubus caesius — Dewberry	■			■					
R. fruiticosus — Bramble	■								
R. ulmifolius — Bramble ssp.			■						
Rumex acetosa — Common Sorrel	■	■							
R. acetosella — Sheep's Sorrel	■	■							
R. crispus — Curled Dock	■	■	■						
Sagina apetala — Annual Pearlwort			■						
S. maritima — Sea Pearlwort			■	■					
S. procumbens — Procumbent Pearlwort	■		■						
Sambucus nigra — Elder	■	■							
Sanguisorba minor — Salad Burnet	■								
Scrophularia nodosa — Common Figwort					■				
Sedum acre — Biting Stonecrop	■	■		■					
Senecio bicolor — Silver Ragwort									■

118

		1890	1932	1963	1967	1979	1983	1986	1987	1988
S. jacobaea	Common Ragwort									
S. vulgaris	Groundsel									
Sherardia arvensis	Field Madder									
Silene vulgaris	Bladder Campion									
S. maritima	Sea Campion									
Sinapis arvensis	Charlock									
Sisymbrium officinale	Hedge Mustard									
Smyrnium olusatrum	Alexanders									
Solanum dulcamara	Bittersweet									
S. nigrum	Black Nightshade									
Sonchus asper	Prickly Sow-thistle									
S. oleraceus	Smooth Sow-thistle									
Stachys palustris	Marsh Woundwort									
Stellaria media	Common Chickweed									
S. pallida	Lesser Chickweed									
Syringa vulgare	Lilac									
Tamus communis	Black Briony									
Tanacetum vulgare	Tansy									
Taraxacum officinale	Common Dandelion									
Teucrium scorodonia	Wood Sage									
Thymus praecox	Wild Thyme									
T. serpyllum	Breckland Thyme									
Tragopogon pratensis	Goat's-beard									
Trifolium campestre	Hop Trefoil									
T. dubium	Lesser Trefoil									
T. medium	Zig-zag Clover									
T. micranthum	Slender Trefoil									
T. ornithopioides	Bird's-foot Clover									
T. pratense	Red Clover									
T. repens	White Clover									
T. scabrum	Rough Clover									
Tussilago farfara	Colt's-foot									
Umbilicus rupestris	Navelwort									
Urtica dioica	Common Nettle									
U. urens	Small Nettle									
Verbascum thapsus	Great Mullein									
Veronica agrestis	Green Field-speedwell									
V. arvensis	Wall Speedwell									
V. chamaedrys	Germander Speedwell									
V. persica	Common Field-speedwell									
V. polita	Grey Field-speedwell									
V. serpyllifolia	Thyme-leaved Speedwell									
Vicia hirsuta	Hairy Tare									
V. sativa	Common Vetch									

		1890	1932	1963	1967	1979	1983	1986	1987	1988
V. sativa ssp. nigra	Narrow-leaved Vetch			■					■	
Vinca major	Greater Periwinkle		■				■	■		
Viola hirta	Hairy Violet		■			■		■		
V. riviniana	Common Dog-violet		■							
Zostera marina	Eelgrass	■								
Asplenium adiantum-nigrum	Black Spleenwort								■	■
A. ceterach	Rustyback									
A. marinum	Sea Spleenwort									
A. ruta-muraria	Wall-rue	■								
A. trichomanes	Maidenhair Spleenwort									
Phillitis scolopendrium	Hartstongue									
Pteridium aquilinum	Bracken	■	■	■	■	■	■	■	■	■
Agrostis stonifera	Creeping Bent			■						
A. capillaris	Common Bent			■			■			
Aira caryophyllea	Silver Hair-grass		■	■						
A. praecox	Early Hair-grass			■						
Anthoxanthum odoratum	Sweet Vernal Grass		■	■						
Arrhenatherum elatius	False Oat-grass		■	■	■	■	■	■	■	■
Avenula pubescens	Downy Oat-grass			■						
Brachypodium sylvaticum	False Brome			■						
Briza media	Quaking Grass		■							
Bromus hordaceus ssp. ferronii	Least Soft Brome		■	■						
B. hordaceus ssp. hordaceus	Soft Brome		■							
B. sterilis	Barren Brome		■	■						
Cynosurus cristatus	Crested Dogstail		■							
Dactylis glomerata	Cocksfoot	■	■	■	■	■	■	■	■	■
Desmazeria marina	Sea Fern Grass		■							
D. rigida	Fern Grass			■						
Festuca ovina	Sheep's Fescue		■	■						
F. rubra	Red Fescue		■	■						
Holcus lanatus	Yorkshire Fog		■	■	■	■	■	■	■	■
Koeleria macrantha	Crested Hair-grass		■							
Lolium perenne	Perennial Ryegrass		■							
Phleum pratense	Timothy		■							
P. pratense ssp. bertolonii	Smaller Catstail			■						
Poa annua	Annual Meadow-grass		■	■						
P. pratensis	Smooth Meadow-grass		■				■			
P. subcaerulea	Spreading Meadow-grass		■			■				
P. trivialis	Rough Meadow-grass			■						
Puccinellia maritima	Common Saltmarsh Grass		■							
Trisetum flavescens	Yellow Oat-grass		■	■	■	■				

120

		1890	1932	1963	1967	1979	1983	1986	1987	1988	
Carex caryophyllea	Spring Sedge										
C. echinata	Star Sedge			▓							
C. flacca	Glaucous Sedge			▓							
C. muricata	Prickly Sedge		▓	▓							
C. nigra	Common Sedge										
C. polphylla											

The Wild Peony,
drawn by Lorna Gibson.

121

AFTERWORD on THE KNIGHTS

by Rodney Legg

It is sad to debunk legends, but John Fowles steered me clear of the enduring myths that cling to the two Holms of the Bristol Channel. Having proved to any unbiased person's judgement the utter impossibility of Saint Gildas having actually written his Dark Ages history on Steep Holm, the novelist then demolished the claim of Flat Holm to have two of the bodies of the knights responsible for slaying Thomas Becket, Archbishop of Canterbury, on the High Altar in Canterbury Cathedral.

Earlier in the text I have edited and subdued Bob Jory's enthusiastic repetition of this tradition, by mentioning the inconvenient fact that they have graves elsewhere.

The events of Tuesday 29 December 1170 produced some of the most dramatic dialogue in English history. The sequel was almost instant sainthood for Thomas and a shrine as popular as any in Europe.

Four knights had gone to Canterbury to demand that Thomas carried out King Henry's wishes and gave immediate and unconditional absolution of bishops suspended on the Pope's orders. The four knights were Hugh de Morville, William de Tracy, Reginald Fitznurse, and Richard le Breton. Realising they were armed and menacing, the cathedral attendants moved to bar the door into the north transept. The knights were accompanied by a clerk, Hugh of Horsea.

BECKET, stopping closure of the door: "God's house must be closed against no man."

KNIGHT: "Where is the traitor, Thomas Becket?"

BECKET: "Here I am, not traitor, but Archbishop and priest of God. What seek ye?"

FITZNURSE: "Your death — hence, traitor!"

BECKET: "I am no traitor, and I will not stir hence." With this Fitznurse removed the archbishop's cap with a swipe of his sword.

BECKET: "Wretch!" The other knights moved towards Becket's attendants.

BECKET: "Slay me here, if you will, but touch any of my people you are accursed."

Edward Grim stayed at his side, bearing the cross and preventing the five intruders from dragging the archbishop from the church. Becket maintained his refusal to absolve the bishops. There was a struggle and the knights drew their swords.

BECKET, covering his eyes: "To God and the blessed Mary, to the patron saints of this church and St Denys, I commend myself and the church's cause." (First and second blows to the head.) "Lord, into Thy hands I commend my spirit." (Becket then turned to the altar of St Benedict, to his immediate right.) "For the name of Jesus and for the defence of the Church I am ready to embrace death." (The third sword-stroke sliced the tonsured crown from his skull.)

HUGH OF HORSEA: "Let us be gone. This man will rise up no more."

His spirit and the king's lamentations would cause them to flee for their lives to banishment and penance. That has been linked to a location in the Black Mountains but the four seemed to have removed themselves to Saltwood and South Malling, in Kent, and then Scotland, before taking refuge in Knaresborough Castle, North Yorkshire. This was the home of Hugh de Morville who alone out of the four had refrained from taking a swipe at Becket's head.

This knight accepted and survived the penance of a crusade in the Holy Land, given by the Pope, and died in 1204. He seems to have died at Kirkoswald, Cumberland, but the Flat Holm claim to his body is duplicated by the

Templar church in Jerusalem, subsequently the Mosque el Aksa, with a porch tomb that has been incorporated in the main building.

Hugh's trophy of the infamous day was William de Tracy's sword, which he left to Carlisle Cathedral.

Tracy had died in 1173, at Cosenze in Sicily, while heading for the Holy Land.

The third of the four who has been linked with Flat Holm — there are two graves but three names given to the occupants — was Reginald Fitznurse. He is also said to be buried in Jerusalem "before the door of the Templars' church", but others say he is buried in Ireland and that his descendants there are called McMahon.

So there remains plenty of scope for counter-claims and Flat Holm is as close to ordinary decent obscurity as anywhere.

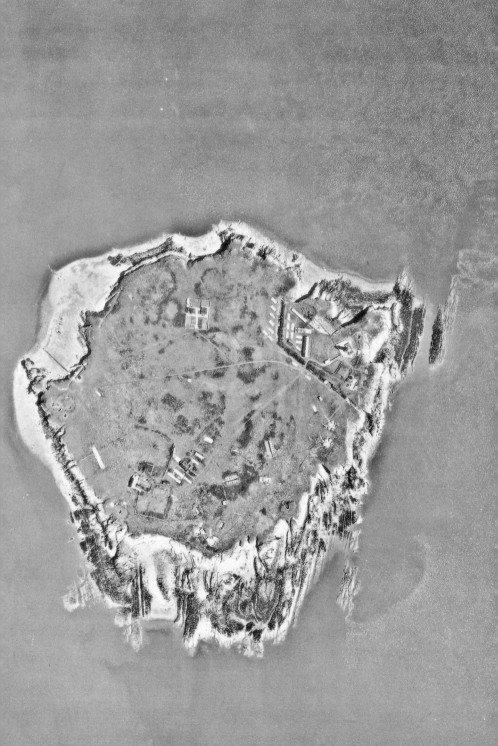

Aerial photographs: vertical reconnaissance (overleaf) with East Beach and the island's northern side bound into the spine of the book. Lighthouse Point is towards the outer edge. In the oblique photograph above, taken from the south-east, the Lighthouse is in the central foreground. Photographs by the Ordnance Survey and Terence Soames Photography.

66, Victoria Street,
London, S.W.

March 30 th 1896.

Dear Mr Preece,

    I am taking the liberty of sending
to you with this note a young Italian of the name
of Marconi, who has come over to this country
with the idea of getting taken up a new system of
telegraphy without wires, at which he has been
working. It appears to be based upon the use of
Hertzian waves, and Oliver Lodge's coherer, but
from what he tells me he appears to have got
considerably beyond what I believe other people
have done in this line.

    It has occurred to me that you
might possibly be kind enough to see him and hear
what he has to say and I also think that what he

has done will very likely be of interest to you.

    Hoping that I am not troubling you too
much.

       Believe me,

       Yours very truly,

       A. A. C. Swinton

W. H. Preece Esq. C.B.

Guglielmo Marconi
101 Hereford Rd
Bayswater Bologna

**Messages across water: Marconi's letter of introduction, in 1896, and
Flat Holm seen from the other side of the main shipping lane of the
Bristol Channel, with shelduck swimming off Steep Holm.
Photographed by Colin Graham in May 1977.**

Post Office inspection: officials G.N. Partridge, H.C. Price, and S.E. Hailes giving serious attention to Marconi's transmitting apparatus and morse inker at Lavernock Point, in May 1897. The first signals across water were duly recorded (opposite). Welsh Industrial and Maritime Museum photographs.

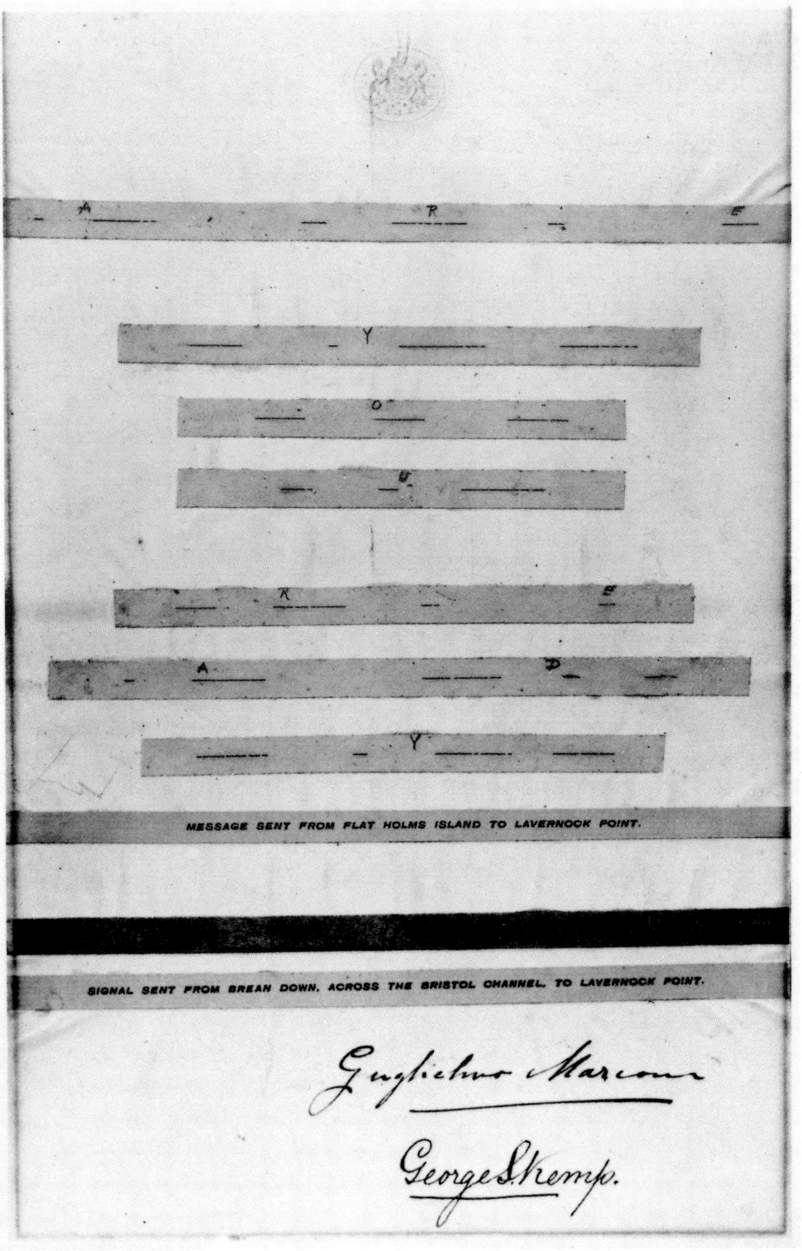

A   R   E

Y

O

U

R   E

A   D

Y

MESSAGE SENT FROM FLAT HOLMS ISLAND TO LAVERNOCK POINT.

SIGNAL SENT FROM BREAN DOWN, ACROSS THE BRISTOL CHANNEL, TO LAVERNOCK POINT.

Guglielmo Marconi

George S. Kemp.

Lighthouse Point: featuring the Lighthouse and ancillary buildings, the Palmerstonian dry moat and two Victorian barbettes, plus the 1941-built Royal Artillery command centre, to the right. Seen in the 1960s. Below, photographed about 1910, is the former Foghorn Station, towards the centre of the island, with compressed-air foghorns.

Opposite: Flat Holm and Lighthouse, seen in the early 1980s, shortly before automation. The view is south-westwards, with the sister island of Steep Holm — just over two miles away — seen in hazy silhouette towards the bottom left. Photographed by Ian C. Bant for the Gordon Frazer Gallery.

Annual picnic: of Weston-super-Mare Swimming Club, who came by boat with some firemen friends (opposite) in 1910. They appear to be above the West Beach, where a winch was used to haul boats above the high-water mark. Locals then and now, especially the boatmen, know the island as 'Flatholms' — as does the sign for the Flatholms Hotel (also opposite). The Holmes was the collective name for the two estuarine islands of the Bristol Channel.

Wartime arrivals: departures first, of some day visitors before the Great War, and then unique photographs (opposite) of the advance party of 930 Port Construction and Repair Company of the Royal Engineers arriving to fortify Flat Holm in July 1941. Their pictures, by sapper Harold Parr, show East Beach from offshore and the 300-ton motor vessel *Assurity*, driven as far up the beach as possible. Her loads of steel girders, for pier-building, were removed as the tide ebbed.

East Beach: wartime steps to a Nissen hut and a boat-haul derrick.
Photographed in about 1950, as was the top photograph opposite. The
landing stage was constructed by Trevor Knowles and Ron Murphy in
the 1960s.

**War-works: Lighthouse and Foghorn Station with 1868-built Barracks
and 1941-added Nissen hut bases between. South Battery and wartime
magazines, constructed by the Royal Engineers with Pioneer Corps
labour, in 1941-42, are seen opposite.**

Farmhouse views: pre-1914 and in 1955 (opposite) with the Cholera
Hospital Laundry in ruins to the left. Above is the island's last private
tenant, R.G. Knowles of Trowbridge, making contact with the mainland
in the 1950s — Marconi's wireless telegraphy now being in daily use.

Ruins rescued: the renovated Farmhouse (left) in 1994, though the Cholera Hospital Laundry still awaits its spring-clean. Behind the Farmhouse a new garden has taken shape, inside the old buttressed walls.

Overleaf: gulls and the vision for the future, with Flat Holm Local
Nature Reserve — created by South Glamorgan County Council — seen
in a watercolour by D. Mayne Stephens of Dinas Powis.

Index